The Internet Marketing Bible

Zeke Camusio

DEDICATION

To Tiana, my wife. Only you know how much dedication and time being a full-time Internet marketer takes. Thank you for being so patient and supportive. I love you.

CONTENTS

INTRODUCTION

As an entrepreneur, I am the first to admit that I've made a lot of mistakes over the years. When I was 17, a customer called me and wanted to buy a product that I knew wasn't right for him. But he wanted it so I sold it to him anyway. My gut told me I shouldn't have sold it to him, because I knew the product would not help him. Sure, I wouldn't have made that $50, but I would have rather earned his respect instead. This was one of most valuable lessons I learned in my life.

When I was 20, my goal was to make $5,000 per month and I made that much after two months. Three years later, I found a mentor who told me I wasn't making more because I didn't want to push myself. "That's ridiculous!" I responded. "Of course I want to make more money." But he was right. I was setting my own limits. I needed to dream bigger. He recommended a book called "The Magic of Thinking Big" which changed my life.

I was on the right path, but I still had difficult lessons to learn. My first companies were a big mess. We didn't have any systems in place. We didn't take a proactive approach to business; we put out fires as they appeared. Now my company is in great shape and very profitable. Everybody is happier and clients are managed better. The best part is that because we have solid systems in place, we can grow our business without having to work harder.

I failed over the years and tried a lot of things that never panned out. But I picked myself up and trudged along. That's the key to my success - I work very hard and never give up. For me, success isn't about making as much money as you possibly can. My motto is make enough money to support the lifestyle you want. I travel the world, play my guitar, practice yoga and Pilates, ski, surf, and play rugby, tennis, soccer, and golf. I read every day, listen to my favorite music, meditate and spend quality time with my wife.

I learned that a simple lifestyle is far more rewarding than working long hours and never having enough time to enjoy my success and the important people in my life. Not to mention, I'm a much happier, relaxed person now.

I don't want entrepreneurs to make the same mistakes I made over the years. I don't want you to spin your wheels and waste your valuable time and energy like I did. This book is all about working smarter and not working harder.

Most online marketing books out there are too technical for the average business owner. They confuse you with big concepts and technical jargon which is an instant turn off to entrepreneurs. In this book, you won't be bored with useless information about "the history of the Internet."

The Internet Marketing Bible is a clutter-free, step-by-step tutorial that gives you practical tools to achieve marketing success. It is the most comprehensive guide to Internet marketing that will help your business grow and thrive. You will learn:

- How to rank your website #1 on Google with search engine optimization

- How to get thousands of visitors from Facebook, Twitter, YouTube and LinkedIn

- How to set up a Google AdWords campaign the way pros do, so you get more qualified traffic for much less than your competitors pay

- How to rank your local business #1 on Google Places and get thousands of dollars worth of business from Google

- How to skyrocket the conversion rate of your site so more visitors become paying customers

- How to use affiliate marketing, email marketing and online advertising to put the right marketing message in front of your targeted audience.

I hope that this book gives you the tools you need to successfully market your business online.

Zeke Camusio
CEO – The Outsourcing Company
www.TheOutsourcingCompany.com

CHAPTER 1

THE BEST MARKETING ADVICE "GURUS" NEVER TELL YOU

Like many of you, I've been skeptical over the years about these big promises marketing "gurus" make. You see their ads plastered all over the Internet preaching instant success. They promise six figure incomes IF you pay them a big chunk of money, and follow their one-of-a-kind marketing strategy.

After you buy their course and follow every step, you realize you wasted your time and money. These "gurus" didn't tell you anything new about marketing. Why does it seem that everyone else has all the answers BUT you? What's the big secret that these "gurus" never tell you?

A few years ago, my friend and I were driving to my tennis club and I saw a huge hair recovery ad on a building. My friend was going bald so I mentioned, "Look, you should try that." He immediately replied, "No, that doesn't work." I asked him if he had ever tried it. He responded that it looked like a bogus ad that promised false results.

That's when it finally clicked with me. I finally understood marketing. My friend was going bald. He would give ANYTHING to get his hair back and money was not an issue for him. The only reason that stopped him from taking the first step was skepticism.

Then it hit me: "Interesting! If skepticism is the problem, then what is the solution?" I realized there are just two secret ingredients you need to kick-start your marketing towards success.

Secret #1 Provide PROOF that your product actually works

By proof, I don't mean an anonymous testimonial from John A., NYC. Proof equates to dozens of "before and after" shots, several video testimonials with full names and cities, bank account statements showing your profits, proof of legal cases you won, etc. Don't just TELL people you're good. Show them that your products actually work for real live, human beings.

Secret #2 Even if your product doesn't work, your customers always come out on top

If you sell pink wigs and you offer a 100 percent money back guarantee, that's not enough. If people don't like your wigs, they just spent their valuable time ordering online. Then they will spend even more time driving to the post office to return the wig.

Who's going to pay the customer for her wasted time? What about the disappointment of getting something that doesn't meet her expectations? How will she be compensated?

In this case, I'd offer a 120 percent money back guarantee and the customer gets to keep the wig. If your product is a high-ticket item, offer a 110 percent money back guarantee, allow people to keep part of the package (i.e. a pillow if they bought a mattress), and you pay for the return shipping. Your prospects should be able to answer a resounding **YES** to this question: "If I don't like this product, will I end up better off than I was before this transaction?"

If you are concerned about losing money by offering an outrageous guarantee, you might not be able to get around people ripping you off. However, if your refunds increase by 25 percent and your sales by 220 percent, doesn't this offer make good business sense? These are actual numbers gathered by one of my favorite direct response marketers.

If you think too many people will ask for a refund based on your product quality, then consider offering a better product or switch to a different industry. You won't get ahead if you continue to sell a mediocre product.

Remember...IF your customer wins, whether or not your product works, AND you put that message directly in front of the right audience...then you have a winning marketing strategy.

Your Secret Ingredient to an Irresistible Marketing Message

Providing proof is just the FIRST step to a winning marketing strategy. Are you tired of pitching to non-responsive prospects? Are you tired of people stopping by your business and leaving two seconds later? If you answered "yes" to the above questions, I can guarantee your marketing message needs a drastic overhaul.

An irresistible marketing message doesn't just happen overnight – forget what the "gurus" have preached to you in the past. Invest time and energy into creating a marketing message that catches your clients' and prospects' attention, and makes them come back for more.

Step 1: Who Is Your Ideal Client?

This is a very important question, because you can't sell to people you don't know anything about. Here are a few sample questions to get you started:

- Is my client a man or a woman?

- What's her age range?

- How much does she make?

- What are the most important things in her life?

- Does she have kids?

- Is she married? What is her relationship like?

- What does my client look like? Is she healthy? What does she eat? Does she exercise?

- Does she have free time? What does she do in her free time?

- What is her average day like? (Describe it in as much detail as you can from beginning to end.)

Step 2: Understanding the Decision-Making Process

There are four roles in a purchasing decision. All four roles can be performed by the same person or by different people.

#1 Researcher - Who researches the different options available?

#2 Decision Maker - Who makes the final decision?

#3 Influencer - Who influences the decision?

#4 User - Who uses the product?

Step 3: Finding Hot Buttons

Let's suppose that you sell software for lawyers. After conducting step two of the above decision-making process, you discover that the lawyer is both the researcher and decision maker. However, his assistant is the influencer and user. You need to sell your software to lawyers and their assistants. They are different people with different motivations. Let's take it one step further…

Why do lawyers want to use your software?

1. Because the software sends automated emails to their clients: they get to bill more hours (which means more money).

2. Because all their contacts are organized: they can waste less time searching for phone numbers (saves time).

3. It saves their assistants time: they can pay them less (saves money).

Why do their assistants want to use your software?

1. It saves them time. As a result, they get to spend more time on Facebook (they can have fun and relax).

2. Automates their daily tasks (ease of use).

Because you're selling to both lawyers and their assistants, include benefits for BOTH in your marketing message. Consider this headline:

"How Lawyers Can Increase Their Income, Work Less and Make Their Assistants Happy"

Step 4: Reaching Your Audience

Based on the research above, you need to reach 35 to 50 year old lawyers (who own their firms) and their assistants. Their assistants are male and female law school students between the ages of 20 and 26.

How can you reach these targeted audiences? Here are five probing questions to consider:

1. What magazines do they read?

2. What websites do they visit?

3. Who are their role models and mentors?

4. What radio shows do they listen to on a regular basis?

5. How do they make their decisions? By recommendation? If so, who do they get recommendations from? How can you reach those people?

Step 5: Do It!

At this point, you know who your ideal client is; how he or she makes their decisions; who else is involved in the decision making process; what motivates these people to take action and how to reach them. Your next step? **DO IT!**

Measure everything you do, find out what works and what doesn't - DO more of what works!

Less is More: Why Word-of-Mouth Marketing Goes a Long Way

As an entrepreneur, I've analyzed hundreds of businesses over the years. As a result, I realize there is ONE crucial indicator that helps me better predict what companies will succeed and what companies will fail. Does word-of-mouth marketing work for their company?

Case #1

You sell a boring, mediocre product. You tell ten people about your product then they tell two more people, but the message dies there.

As a result, you always have to continuously market to your market because people won't spread the word for you. This is known as unilateral marketing.

Case #2

You sell a "buzz worthy" product that everyone wants. You tell ten people about your product. These ten people tell five more people. Now you have fifty total people spreading your message to MORE people and so on. Get the ball rolling and your customers will do the rest.

Case #1 Versus Case #2

In **Case #1**, the company GETS PEOPLE TALKING ABOUT THEM and in **Case #2** the company doesn't – people spread the word. That's it. That's the MOST important marketing lesson I've ever learned.

If you're remarkable, all you need to do is tell a few people about your products and word-of-mouth will do the rest. You won't be able to stop sales from constantly growing no matter how hard you try. On the other hand, if people don't talk about your business you can spend thousands in marketing and your business will never take off. You might retain some customers, but your business becomes a car without an engine. The moment you stop pushing it, your business stops moving forward.

How to Be Remarkable and Make a Lasting Impression

This is my favorite part about marketing: you need to be weird. A great product, at an even better price, just won't do the trick. When I say weird, I don't mean 'crazy' weird. I mean creative and different – when it's time to step outside your marketing comfort zones.

Take a page from these big players. The following companies took weird and different to a new level, and got the entire world talking about them in the process:

Yahoo!

When Yahoo! was ranked as the top search engine, their competitors attempted to beat them by introducing more features and information. Google took it ten steps further and did something outrageous: they offered LESS. They gave Google users less clutter, fewer features and MORE accurate search results.

Twitter

Twitter created a new concept in blogging – posts that cannot exceed 140 characters.

Zappos

This dynamic company revolutionized the shoe industry by offering free rush delivery and returns. Zappos even pays for postage costs if you need to return or exchange a pair of shoes.

Whole Foods

They offered a central location for premium organic foods like no other company has done in the past.

Niche Marketing: Why You Can't Be All Things to All People

Last year I went skiing in Aspen, Colorado with friends. I haven't been on skis since I was two years old. One of them foolishly suggested: "Hey, let's do double back flips." I thought he was kidding…I was wrong!

We hit the slopes and watched as my friends performed amazing double back flips. Then it was my turn and I was completely terrified. My heart was beating so hard it almost broke my ribs. Then my friends starting calling me "chicken" (yes, they knew how to push my buttons) so I decided to just go for it. I love a challenge and this was a big one.

As you can imagine, I didn't land the double back flip. I hit my back so hard I could barely breathe. Luckily, I didn't break anything, but one month later my back was still in a lot of pain.

As a result of my back pain, I started searching for doctors and found a newspaper ad that caught my eye:

Ski-Related Back Injury? I'll make your pain go away in 3 weeks or you pay nothing.

I thought, "Wow! This doctor read my mind." The guarantee was great, but the fact that she treated back pain caused by ski wrecks was even more impressive. It was like she wrote the ad just for me.

There were other ads from doctors that promised to make pain disappear, but nobody talked about back injuries - let alone ski-related back injuries. Who do you think I called?

Why You Should Position Yourself as a Specialist

- **Higher Perceived Value**
  When you're the "tax consultant who does taxes for small business owners in the health industry," your services have a much higher perceived value than those from "that person who does taxes for the entire planet."

- **Charge More Money**
  I was more than happy to pay a higher premium for my back

pain specialist. I paid about 30 percent more than the average doctor visit but that seemed like a bargain.

- **Less Competition (or No Competition at All)**
  How many doctors do you know who specialize in back pain caused by ski injuries? I'm guessing very few. If I ever hurt my back again, this is the only doctor I'd ever consider seeing.

- **Easier to Find Your Target Market**
  My doctor was born in Chicago, but there isn't much skiing there. She focused on a targeted market: injured skiers with back pain from Aspen, Colorado. Smart, huh? When you find a niche market, finding your customers who want and need your products/services is a piece of cake.

- **Push Your Customers' Hot Buttons**
  When you find a niche market, you can tailor your marketing message to say exactly what your market wants to hear.

- **Inexpensive Marketing Channels**
  My doctor uses two marketing channels: newspaper ads and a sign on Aspen's hospital billboard. That's it. When people become injured, they go to the hospital. While they wait, they're exposed to the billboard. They're bored and then read the sign. Genius marketing!

How to Successfully Tap into Sub-Niche Marketing

If you think niche marketing is a great idea, but you are worried about leaving out 90 percent of the market then "sub-niche" marketing is the way to go. Split your business and separate your target niches into different categories.

Sub-niche marketing worked well for my client:

- Company ABC offers golf tours for seniors, field hockey tours for women, and rugby tours for men in New Zealand.

- They had their three niches under one website which wasn't working well.

- When I started working with Company ABC, we created three websites – one for each niche market.

- Their three niche markets were very different and needed different marketing approaches. We then wrote new copy for each niche.

Customers chose Company ABC who specializes in three separate tours to New Zealand. Since I went after three niches and then created three separate websites, their customer inquiries increased by 250 percent. Instead of marketing Company ABC as a general tour company who tried to be everything to EVERYONE, we zeroed into each niche that better served their specific markets.

Why Bigger Works Better Sometimes

The goal is to concentrate on smaller, niche markets, but that does NOT work all the time. Friends and colleagues come to me over and over again with the same complaint: "Am I EVER going to make money?" They are frustrated because their businesses don't make the kind of money they thought they would make.

I find myself asking them the same questions, which resulted in the same answer: their niche markets were small and their gross profits per sales were extremely low.

When you go after a tiny niche market and only make $20 per sale, that's not exactly a winning sales model. However, that's what most "wannabe" Internet marketers do. But why do they continue to do it? Because that's what these "gurus" teach them to do.

"Gurus" preach two marketing concepts:

#1 Market to small, defined niches because there is less competition.

#2 Sell eBooks because they are easy money.

There are two big issues with this type of advice when it comes to your sales. A small market means less people to sell your products to. If you want to make $10,000 per month, you'll need to sell 500 eBooks at $20 each. Making $500 in sales in a small niche is not easy and won't last long. If your market is too small and you sell products too cheaply, you'll never make any money. It goes back to "work smarter not harder."

Here's an inside tip that most people don't know about. Even though they preach selling to smaller niches, these "gurus" don't follow their own advice. They make their six-figure incomes selling to Internet marketing wannabes which is a HUGE market. These "gurus" are smart and they know how to sell. First, they sell e-books – the entry point of their sales funnel. Once Internet marketers are in their sales funnel, they sell DVDs, seminar tickets and one-on-one coaching sessions.

Making BIG things happen takes work – a LOT of work! Don't think about HOW much money you are going to make. Turn things around and put yourself in the shoes of your customers. Ask yourself this question: **"Am I giving my customers a lot more in value than what they pay for my products?"** That's how you build a strong business: by helping improve people's lives. But remember

– if you're in business just for the money, your customers will notice it.

It is perfectly acceptable to think BIG sometimes when it comes to your target markets:

- The larger the market, the more people to sell products to.

- You can have low-ticket items to engage people into your sales funnel, but make sure you have high-ticket products to offer down the road.

- Offer a great solution to a painful problem AND the money will follow.

Ask and You Shall Receive: Why Clients Are Your Best Research Tool

Sometimes we become so immersed in the latest marketing advice from business gurus that we forget to implement the most basic market research tool – surveys. Clients are your bread and butter, but why do you often forget about them?

When was the last time you called your customers and asked them about their experience with your company? When you lose prospects to your competition, do you call them to find out why they didn't choose your company?

If you don't ask the WHYs, you will never figure out what went wrong and why you lost clients. You can have the greatest marketing tricks up your sleeve, but client surveys are one of your most vital market research tools. A few simple probing questions can be the difference between retaining thousands of dollars worth of business OR losing thousands.

Here are key questions I ask clients who left our company and prospects that went with our competition.

Current Clients

1. When you decided to hire us, had you considered other options? If so, why did you choose us?

2. How satisfied are you with the way you performed in that area? (If they tell you they chose your company because of its customer service, ask them how they would rate your customer service).

3. If we could do one thing different to increase your satisfaction level, what would this be?

4. How likely are you to recommend us to your friends and colleagues?

Clients Who Stopped Working with You and Went with Your Competition

1. Why did you decide to stop working with us?

2. What could we have done to prevent this?

Prospects Who Used Your Competition

1. What did you like about our proposal?

2. What didn't you like about our proposal?

3. What areas in Company XYZ's proposal were better?

4. What were the top factors that made you choose Company XYZ over us?

Be Courteous

Remember that busy professionals have better things to do than answer your questions, so remember to ask nicely. Explain that their input will mean a lot to you. If they agree to answer your questions, don't be pushy. Let them know that it is not mandatory to answer all your questions. As a courtesy for answering your questions, send them a thank you letter or a small gift.

Why You Need Client Feedback

Before you jump into your marketing efforts, step back and evaluate by asking your clients and prospects the above questions. How much could you improve your company if you knew exactly why your clients do business with you and why other clients don't? You can spend years wasting your time by trial-and-error OR simply pick up the phone and JUST ASK!

Ten Minute Marketing Checklist

Are you ready to take your business from ordinary to REMARKABLE?

I promise that if you just take ten minutes to think about these marketing tools discussed in Chapter One, they'll be the best ten minutes you ever invested.

1. Are you missing these TWO secret ingredients to your marketing strategy?

- Provide proof that your product actually works

- Even if your product doesn't work, your customers always come out on top

2. Do you know your targeted audiences and decision makers?

3. How will you market your company in a "weird" (but great) way?

4. What will you DO to get raving fans to spread the word about your business?

5. How can you make a difference in the world instead of being JUST another company in your industry?

CHAPTER 2

TOTAL WEBSITE MAKEOVER: HOW TO TRANSFORM AN UNDERPERFORMING SITE INTO YOUR MOST EFFECTIVE SELLING MACHINE

Your website is one of your most effective selling tools, but most people think they can just design an attractive site that sells itself. Yes, a web designer can make your site look good, but don't rely on your designer to do all the work for you. You are responsible for your website marketing.

The Psychology Behind Marketing

The best online marketers I know are observant of human behavior and always keep their eyes open. They notice how people make decisions, and how innovative companies are when it comes to selling their products and services. This is not something that even the best business school can teach you. This is what gives the best marketers in the world an edge over their competitors.

1. Consistency

In *Influence: The Psychology of Persuasion* by Robert Cialdini, he asked a group of people to put a huge sign in their yards with the phrase: "Drive slowly; kids playing." An overwhelming majority of people would not display the sign in their yard. A second group of people were asked to put a tiny sticker in their windows with the same phrase. Almost everyone agreed. They were then asked to put a giant sign in their yards, and a large percentage agreed.

As a result of Cialdini's study, he concluded that people are consistent with their previous actions. If they said yes to something in the past, they are more likely to say yes to it in the future. Let's take a look at how this theory applies to the sales funnel.

2. The Sales Funnel

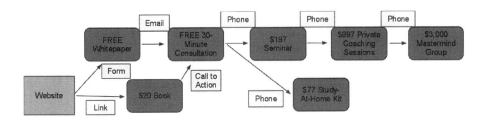

The biggest mistake you can make is to ASSUME every person is ready to buy when they visit your website. Only five to ten percent of website visitors are ready to actually buy your product or service. The sales funnel below shows you how you can turn your visitors into paying customers:

The sales funnel begins with visitors checking out your site. Remember that not everyone is ready to buy at that exact moment.

When visitors enter your sales funnel, offer them a freebie and don't hit them up to buy something right away– take them to the next level. Don't take them from "hey, here's your free white paper!" to "do you want to buy our $3,000 master mind group package?" You need to first build trust and rapport which does not happen overnight.

- **Step One** – For example, Mr. Smith visits your website, Dynamo Coaching. He notices you have a free whitepaper and a $20 book for sale. He decides to download the free whitepaper and fill outs a form which captures his email.

- **Step Two** – Mr. Smith is now on board with your sales funnel. After downloading the whitepaper, he receives your email offering a FREE 30 minute consultation. Because of your strong call to action, Mr. Smith contacts you immediately and takes advantage of your free offer and signs up for your consultation.

- **Step Three** – Mr. Smith is so impressed with his free consultation that he signs up for your $197 seminar.

- **Step Four** – He is now a bona fide paying customer. He sees real worth in your products and services – why he keeps buying from you. As you chat with him on the phone, you tell him about your $997 private coaching sessions which he purchases right on the spot.

- **Step Five** - After Mr. Smith completes his private coaching sessions with you, he tells you on the phone that he was pleased with the coaching he received. You pitch him your $3,000 mastermind group which he purchases.

The sales funnel took Mr. Smith from a curious website visitor to one of your best paying customers who found a valuable investment in Dynamo Coaching's products and services.

3. Contrast and Decoy Offers

The principle of contrast states: "People see things as good or bad depending on what's around them." For example, an ordinary house looks beautiful next to an ugly one, but the same house looks less attractive next to an opulent mansion.

With contrast and decoy offers, include a bad offer on your website. I proved this to be true every time I tested it. It makes your main offer look much better. One of my clients sold four bottles of his product for $89. I added an option to the site - one bottle for $75. His sales for the 4 bottle package increased by approximately 60 percent. Decoy offers make "the real offer" (4 bottles for $89) look very good.

4. Social Validation

People want to be liked and want others to think they make smart decisions. Explain why buying your product is a SMART decision. People need to justify their actions with others and they'll repeat whatever you say.

Make a compelling argument so people feel good about buying your products and services. And make sure whatever you sell is the best of the BEST!

5. High Price = High Quality

Have you noticed that when you go to the $1,000 doctor you feel a lot better than when you go to the $500 doctor? The $300 pair of shoes is always better than pair of $150 shoes? Really? No, not really. It comes down to perceptions and not facts.

You hurt yourself by charging too little for your products and services. Raise your prices and increase the perceived value of your products and services.

6. Exclusivity

People want what they can't have. What restaurant would you rather choose - the one that is booked for the next 3 months or the one that's empty? What school do you want your children to attend - the one with the six month waiting list or the one that advertises open spots for students?

Make sure your prospects know you don't just take "anyone" as a client. Tell them they need to apply and you select clients that are a good fit. This will make them want you even more!

If you sell products and you don't think you can pull this off, tell people why they SHOULDN'T buy your product. For example, if you sell handmade lamps, use the following twist in your copy: "If you're looking for cheap lamps, you won't find them here. If you're the kind of person who appreciates artistic lamps hand-made by Asian artisans, you're in the right place."

7. Too Many Choices = No Action

Doesn't it frustrate you when you want to buy a digital camera, but when you visit eBay they have 3,497,765 cameras listed? It will take you all day to find a camera!

Narrow down the choices you give your visitors. Limited choices increase your sales potential because people are more apt to buy from a smaller range of choices.

8. Scarcity

People take action when the offer might not be available in the future. Giving people reasons to act isn't enough. You need to tell them exactly why they need to act NOW!

Examples:

- This offer expires on Friday!

- I'll only be teaching this teleclass to 10 people.

- I'll take only one client this week.

- Only 4 items available. When they're gone, they're gone forever!

9. Risk Reversal

The lower the risk an action has, the higher the chance someone will take action. Include a guarantee, but go beyond the standard "money back guarantee."

- If you don't lose 5 lbs. in 10 days with my personal training program, I won't charge you a dime, I'll train you for free for an extra month and I'll even pay for your gym membership.

- If your back keeps hurting after trying the BackGenius 2500, just give us a call and we'll give you 200% of your money back, pay for the return shipping and we'll even take care of the pick up.

Guarantee results not just "satisfaction." Be very specific. Depending on your market, about one percent of people will rip you off, BUT your sales will double. Do the math and see if it works out for you. Hint: it will ALWAYS work out in your favor.

Your market is going to be taken by the boldest marketers. This could be you or your competitors. Don't let fear stop you from winning. If you are afraid things will go south, just test your guarantee on 200 sales and keep some reserve cash just in case. Then compare the extra sales with the refunds you give back, and see if it makes sense to continue doing it.

Website "Makeover" Tips

I learned over the years that people can be overly sensitive when it comes to their websites. I remember one client in particular told me to take a hike. He adamantly disagreed with my website suggestions (which were based on solid metrics and research), yet he still didn't want to listen to my advice.

Don't let stubborn pride get in the way of making money from your site. You could lose out on huge sales as a result of an underperforming site. The following "makeover" tips show you how to transform your mediocre website into an effective selling machine.

People make a lot of mistakes when it comes to their websites – from complicated navigation to poor copy. Does your website need an overhaul? Keep these tips in mind as you review your website.

Tip #1 Make Your Site Web 3.0 Ready

- Allow visitors to subscribe by RSS and email

- Allow visitors to follow you through social media - Facebook, Twitter and LinkedIn

- Allow visitors to share content through social media (Facebook and Twitter) and email (include "Share" plug-ins, such as ShareThis.com)

Tip #2 Don't Get Too Clever With Your Site

Make your site look professional and appealing, but don't be too creative. A website is a marketing tool so you want the site to be easy to navigate so visitors take action. Don't clutter your website with too many images, buttons, etc. Less is more - stick to a clean website that simply says who you are, who you serve, and what you do.

Tip #3 Don't Ask For More Information Than You Really Need

People become frustrated when they have to fill out lengthy contact forms, so keep it simple. If you only need basic contact information, just ask for name and email.

Tip #4 Make it Easy for People to Contact You

Make it easy for people to get in touch with you. Include your contact form on every page of your site.

Tip #5 Monetize Your Site

- Sell your own products

- Sell someone else's products

- Sell leads

- Sell ads

- Ask for donations

Tip #6 Use Credible Testimonials and Expert Endorsements

The sales funnel I mentioned earlier is a good example of how to gain visitors' trust from the beginning and turn them into paying customers. However, another powerful way to gain trust from people is through credible testimonials and expert endorsements on your site.

The sad truth about testimonials is that many people make them up, and they sound fake. Use the person's first and last name so it sounds legitimate - don't use "Suzy Q., California." Summarize your testimonials. People don't have time to read long-winded testimonials.

Include your client list/logos, certifications, awards, trust logos (i.e. "PayPal Verified"), credentials, etc. in order to showcase your expertise and credibility. Celebrity and expert endorsements can further enhance your credibility. You don't need Donald Trump to vouch for you (although, that would be nice), but industry experts who endorse your products and services can go a long way.

Tip #7 Include Case Studies

One of your best-selling tools is case studies. It's all about proof and evidence. Show people real proof of how you can help them. Many of my clients chose to work with my company as a result of reading our case studies on our site. Here is an example of my client's case study:

Case Study #1: "First on Yahoo in Only 3 Months"

The Website: EnglishLCI.com

The Problems:

They were #154 on Yahoo for their main keyword: "Learn English in Denver".

All their competitors appeared in Google Maps but they didn't.

What We Did:

We fixed a few big issues they had in their website architecture.

We optimized their tags and content.

We built over 850 high-quality links from relevant sites using relationship marketing and advanced content syndication tactics.

The Results:

Our client is now first on Yahoo and Google Maps for their main keyword.

Their traffic doubled in only 3 months.

The Proof:

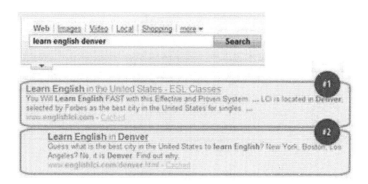

They have the #1 and #2 positions for this keyword.

They are also #1 on Google Maps.

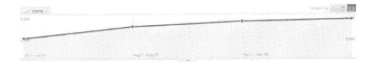

Their traffic doubled (from 2,307 to 4,670) in only 3 months.

Tip #8: Write Strong Copy

You don't need to be a professional copywriter to write effective copy, but you do need to first understand basic copywriting techniques. Don't skimp on good copy. You could have the best website design, but if your copy is lousy then visitors won't stick around. If copywriting isn't your area of expertise, hire a professional copywriter.

- **Use "Conversational Style" Copy**
  Persuade people with strong arguments. Write as you talk; avoid complicated "corporate" jargon that people don't understand.

- **Make Copy Easy to Read**
  Most people will skim through copy so make it easy to read:

  - Use short sentences

  - Use short paragraphs (2-3 sentences)

  - Use lists and bullet points

  - Write at a 5th grade level

  - Use simple words

- **Avoid Adjectives**
  Use strong verbs and power words instead. These are some of my favorite power words: you, satisfied, respected, knowledgeable, humiliate, outraged, pissed off, crave, squeeze, steal, stumble, shock, cured, astonished, killer, miracle, suffocate, liar, bribe, lure, rocked, infested, bandit, abandon, slaughter, tickle, inflame, coax, tease, blast, ridicule, slay, boost, implode, anger, wealthy, ecstasy, heaven, delighted

- **Know Your Target Audience**
  Before you write copy, you need to understand your audience first. Get inside their head and figure out who they are, what they want, need, etc. For more tips, refer back to Chapter One – Who is Your Ideal Client?

- **Talk to Your Salespeople**
  Talk to your sales and customer service staff. How can you write copy geared towards customers if you don't know anything about them? What do people complain about? What are the most common objections your staff receives from prospects?

- **Visit Online Forums**
  Visit online forums and find out what people say. What questions do they ask? What words do they use to describe their problems, frustrations, etc.?

- **Include Risk-Reversal Tactics**
  Make a guarantee so good that even if your product doesn't work, your customer ends up winning. You could offer a 110 percent money back guarantee plus free return shipping, or allow customers to keep part of your kit for having tried your product.

- **Test the Price**

  You won't know how much to charge until you test the price. If you charge too much or too little, you leave money on the table. Use prices ending in 7 (i.e. $17, $27, $39.97). To test prices, start low and increase from there. When total revenues decrease, go back to the original price that worked the best.

- **Up-Sell and Cross-Sell**

  Up-selling is upgrading an order (i.e. "Get the Premium Version for $5 More") and cross-selling is offering related items. For example, if you sell customers digital cameras then sell them a case and extra batteries.

- **Use Benefits, Not Features**

  Focus on the benefits and not the features of your product. A feature is a characteristic of that product, and a benefit is how that feature helps your customer. For example: A camera has a 10x digital zoom (feature). This feature allows you to take close-up photos of small objects from a block away (benefit).

- **Be Specific**

  Specific data is more believable than general data. Don't use: "Studies show that people taking this pill lose a lot of weight." This sounds better: "A study conducted in 2008 by ABC Labs Inc. shows that people lost an average of 7.32 lbs. in 8 days from taking this pill." Do not create false data; back up your data with real facts and show evidence.

- **Include Call to Action**

  Tell people why they need to take action NOW! A call to action stands out and grabs people's attention quickly. "Download your FREE whitepaper now!" sounds decisive and doesn't leave them guessing as to what action they should take.

Words such as "now" and "today" give visitors a sense of urgency. They will then take action and download the whitepaper immediately. Include scarcity statements such as: "limited time" or "limited quantity." People will buy your product since it won't be available for long.

- **Use Social Proof to Overcome Objections**
  Find out what the most common objections are from your customers. Then use testimonials, case studies and expert reviews to overcome those objections. If one of the most common objections from people is that if your product doesn't work they won't receive a refund. In order to resolve that objection, include testimonials on your site from customers who received fast refunds.

- **Stay Positive**
  Maintain a positive tone with your copy. If you sell an acne treatment cream, write about how beautiful your customer's skin looks. Don't focus on how blemished their skin looks. Use positive photos as testimonials to back up your copy.

- **Headlines Are Everything**
  If you can't quickly engage people with your headline, then you will lose them. That's why top copywriters write 50 to 100 headlines before picking a winner.

First, I go to my swipe file and adapt my 100 plus headlines of my products. Put together your own swipe file. Every time you come across a great headline that makes you read the rest of the copy, save it.

I then write 50 headlines combining the different tactics I previously used. I choose four and split-test them – that's how I find a winner. I write variations of that headline and try to beat it. It's a fun game, and some headlines can increase conversions by over 100 percent.

- **Headline that includes three main benefits of your product:**

- "All the Cars in One Place, the Lowest Prices in Town and FREE Lifetime Guarantee"

- **"How to" headline:**

- "How to Get Rid of Acne in 6 Weeks Using Stuff You Already Have in Your Own Kitchen"

- **"Qualifier" headline:**

- "If Your Car Insurance is from Geico, This Letter Is for You"

- **"News" headline:**

- "82-Year-Old Dutch Woman Accidentally Discovers Acne Cure While Cooking Lunch for Her Grandson"

- **Follow a Logical Path**
Copy should flow smoothly from beginning to end. Make sure each link of the copy chain is connected with the links that come right before and after it.

- **First Paragraph**
In the first paragraph you need to say who you are and why you're writing. Sound like a viable expert, and tell them why they need to listen to you and believe what you say.

- **Don't Preach to the Choir**
Don't tell people about their problems; they know them better than you do. "I know how you feel. Acne is awful.

Waking up every day and having to walk around with an acne face is not fun." What's the point? People who suffer from acne don't need to be reminded that it's awful and not fun. They just want you to help them get rid of it.

- **Ask Two People to Read Your Copy Out Loud**
  By asking two objective people to read your copy aloud, this will help you identify the areas where copy doesn't flow well.

How to Create Killer Landing Pages

Understanding how to build effective landing pages will further enhance your marketing message. A landing page is the page that opens when a visitor clicks on a text link, advertisement or search engine result link. Most people send their visitors to their home page, but that's not always a good idea.

These are examples of "good" and "bad" landing pages:

BAD Landing Page

(Too much clutter, not a clear call to action)

GREAT Landing Page

(Clean, clear call to action, stunning graphics and a list of their clients)

Not all visitors are the same. If you sell a $29 book and a $5,000 coaching program, both audiences are very different from each other and need unique marketing approaches. Create a marketing message around a specific call to action, and you will get a much better response with landing pages.

Keep Them Short

Write a powerful headline that attracts immediate attention. Use bulleted lists for your benefits and include a clear call to action. That's it – keep it short and to the point.

Keep Important Information "Above the Fold"

"Above the fold" means "what you can see on your website without having to scroll down." Get rid of huge logos. It's not about your company; it's about your visitors. The three most important elements mentioned above - headline, benefits and call to action -need to stay "above the fold."

Make Sure Copy Flows Well

Copy needs to follow a logical path. First, show the problem. Second, give them a solution to that problem. Lastly, tell people how to take action. Refer to Copywriting Tips in the previous section.

Have ONE Prominent Call to Action

If you ask people to take ten different actions, you'll lose them. Ask for ONE action - make sure your call to action is the focal point of your landing page. Are you tired of seeing those big, red animated arrows showing you where you need to click? Do you know why they are so in your face? Because they actually work!

Include Testimonials

As mentioned before, it's important to include testimonials on your website. It's just as important to include testimonials on your landing pages. What are the most objections people have about your product? Use testimonials to overcome those objections.

Make Your Message Consistent

If your Google AdWords ad reads "Get a FREE Trial" and your landing page features the paid version, you will immediately turn people off. Make sure you have a consistent message throughout your marketing path.

Get Rid of Distractions

You don't need a navigation menu or links to other pages on your site. Define your sales funnel and stick to it. If you absolutely need to display more information, create links that open in new windows.

Don't Ask Too Much from People

Just like websites, don't ask for too much information on landing pages. Avoid long forms and do not ask for any sensitive information (credit card number, social security number, etc.) If you need confidential information, ask for an email and name on the landing page and then ask for the rest of the information in the next step. If people don't complete the entire process, at least you have their contact information and will contact them later.

Credibility and Risk Reversal

As I pointed out earlier, show people why they should trust you. Use case studies, expert endorsements and before/after photos to back up your claims - think "guarantee." Show people how they'll come out on top even if your product doesn't work for them.

Privacy Issues

A simple line that reads: "We hate SPAM as much as you do. We won't send you junk mail and we won't give your address to anyone" should be enough.

Test, Test and More Tests

There is no way to know for sure what headlines, marketing tools and calls to action will work best UNLESS you test them. Use Google Website Optimizer (https://www.google.com/analytics/siteopt/splash?hl=en) to test the most important elements of your website and landing page.

Test your website usability with **Google Analytics** (http://www.google.com/analytics/index.html). Check out this Usability demonstration - *Rocket Surgery Made Easy* by Steve Krug (http://www.youtube.com/watch?v=QckIzHC99Xc) Refer to Chapter 7 for more detailed information about Google Analytics.

Ten Minute "Total Website Makeover" Website Checklist

Take ten minutes to review these questions. Does your website need a "total makeover?"

Marketing

- Do you have credible testimonials and expert endorsements?
- Does every web page have a call to action that stands out?

Social Media

- Can your visitors subscribe to your site by RSS and email?
- Do you have "share" buttons on every page so visitors can easily share content with others?

Design

- Are there elements on your site you could remove?
- Is your copy easy to read and understand?

Testing & Usability

Have you installed Google Analytics and Google Website Optimizer?

CHAPTER 3

SEARCH ENGINE OPTIMIZATION: HOW TO RANK #1 ON GOOGLE

What Is Search Engine Optimization (SEO)?

Important note: To understand the big picture of SEO, you can watch this webinar I did: http://vimeo.com/20933320 The password is "zeke".)

Millions of people use Google every day to search for everything from "diabetes treatment" to "sporting goods store in Chicago." Visitors click on the first results Google returns; nobody cares about page 20 on Google.

Search engine optimization (SEO) is a collection of tactics that help sites rank in Google's first position for search terms that describe their business and/or website. For example, an Italian restaurant in Seattle will benefit from being #1 on Google for search terms like "Seattle Italian restaurant" or "Italian restaurant in Seattle."

SEO is crucial when it comes to your Internet marketing success. If you take SEO seriously, plan on doing it for a few years. However, you can really mess up SEO if you don't know what you're doing. Doing SEO is like fixing a broken car. You need to know what's broken first before you can fix it.

Remember that SEO doesn't magically happen and you won't rank #1 in Google overnight. You need to first spend time building an organic SEO campaign, and you need the right tools to make SEO successfully work. In this chapter, I will walk you through six SEO steps that will help rank your site #1 in Google.

1. **Keyword Research** – Keyword discovery and analysis

2. **Competitive Analysis** – How to find out what areas work and what areas need improvement

3. **On-Page Optimization** – How to create website copy and tags that are keyword-rich

4. **Content Creation** – How to create optimized content

5. **Link Building** – How to get websites to link to your site (links are seen by search engines as votes)

6. **Analytics** – The best tools to analyze and improve your SEO

Step #1 Keyword Research

The first place to start is keyword research. People literally waste years on keyword research. The worst mistake you can make is researching the wrong keywords. You won't ever find "perfect" keywords, but you can get close – if you know what you're doing. Keyword research involves two steps: discovery and analysis.

Step 1 - Keyword Discovery

Google Keyword Tool
https://adwords.google.com/select/KeywordTool?forceLegacy=true

Type your website URL into the Google Keyword Tool - allows you to discover keywords within your web pages. You can also type in your competitor's URL and search for their keywords. Type your keywords into the Keyword Tool, and Google gives suggestions for relevant/higher ranking words.

Let's work with the keyword example mentioned below: "Italian restaurant in Seattle." According to Google, all variations of "Italian restaurant in Seattle" have over 14,000 total searches per month.

Keywords	Advertiser Competition ⑦	Local Search Volume: February ⑦
Keywords related to term(s) entered - sort by relevance ⑦		
italian restaurants seattle		6,600
italian restaurant seattle		5,400
italian restaurants in seattle		1,300
italian restaurant in seattle		590

Check Out Your Competitor's Keywords

Type your competitor's website URL into Google. Review their homepage title (which appears in Google's browser) to find keywords. Then look at their page code. You will find keywords in their meta tags and meta descriptions; this is an easy way to find out what keywords your competitors use.

Step 2 - Keyword Analysis

Broad and Long-Tail Keywords

After finding your keywords, analyze them and see where they rank. For SEO to effectively work, include both broad and long-tail keywords. As outlined in the diagram below, broad keywords bring you more traffic (80%), but your traffic is less targeted and you have lower conversion rates. For example, "dog food" is a broad keyword.

Long-tail keywords are more defined. They bring in less traffic (20%) but the traffic is more targeted and brings higher conversion rates. "Organic dog food" is an example of a long-tail keyword. Be more specific with your long-tail keywords: "food for French bulldogs." Long-tail keywords don't have high search volumes, so fewer people do SEO for them. Thus, they aren't as competitive and it's easier to rank for long-tail keywords.

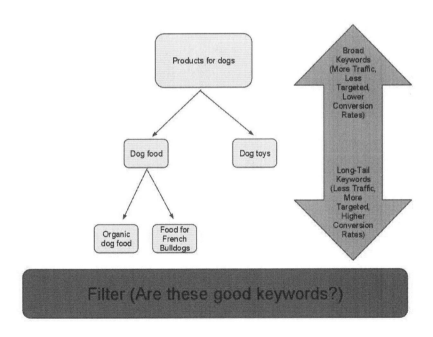

Criteria for Keyword Analysis:

- **Search Volume** – How many people search for these keywords?

- **Relevancy** – How likely will people buy your product? If you sell ergonomic chairs, the keyword "back pain" is not as qualified as "ergonomic chair" (which is extremely relevant).

- **Ranking** – What is the rank for this keyword? If you analyze two keywords, one keyword ranks 500 and the second keyword ranks 11 in Google. Use the second keyword because it ranks #11 (and is closer to Google's first page).

- **Difficulty** – The more difficult the keyword, the worse the keyword. You will probably rank higher in Google if you use "dog owners in New York City" compared to just using "dogs" as a keyword.

There is not ONE perfect keyword formula in the world. However, it is helpful to use the above criteria when analyzing keywords.

If you make a strong commitment to SEO and want to be successful, Pay Per Click (PPC) campaigns such as Google AdWords (http://www.google.com/ads/adwords2/) is one of the best tools for keyword analysis.

Google AdWords looks at your traffic (how many people visit your site) and conversion rates. For example, you might assume that "dog training products" is a good keyword. But when you further analyze the keyword, you realize the keyword converts low on your site.

Keyword Mapping

Keyword	URL 1	URL 2
tennis rackets	Tennis Rackets Page (existing)	
soccer balls	Soccer Balls Page (existing)	
sporting goods	Home Page (existing)	sporting-goods.html
affordable sporting goods	affordable-sporting-goods.html	
denver sporting goods	Home Page (existing)	denver-sporting-goods.html

For every keyword on the first page of Google, optimize at least one page of your site using that keyword. Use an Excel spreadsheet to assist you (see diagram above). For this website, I used the existing "Tennis Rackets Page" (keyword: tennis rackets). I did not have a page for "affordable sporting goods" so I created an optimized page for that keyword.

Step #2 Competitive Analysis

Important note: Watch this competitive analysis webinar I did: http://www.theoutsourcingcompany.com/blog/internet-marketing-events/free-webinar-competitive-analysis-for-seo/

Imagine you drive to a small town you never visited before and you don't have a map, GPS device, Internet access and can't ask people for directions. It would be really difficult to get to that town, wouldn't it? That's how most people conduct their SEO. They don't have a map to see where they are headed and how to arrive at their final destination.

That's not a smart way to tackle SEO, and that's where competitive analysis comes in handy. These are the factors you need to analyze and improve your Google rankings.

- **Number of Indexed Pages**

   Why It's Important: You want search engines to index as many pages of your site as possible.

   How You Can Check this Metric: Use SEOQuake (http://www.seoquake.com) to see how many pages are indexed in Google. Compare your number to your top 10 Google rankings for the keyword you're going after.

   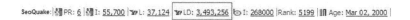

   What to Do About This: If you find that your top 10 competitors have more indexed pages than you, create more pages of optimized content. They could be blog posts, articles, resources, etc.

- **Number of Incoming Links**

   Why It's Important: You want a lot of great incoming links.

   How You Can Check this Metric: Use SEOQuake to see how many incoming links you and your top 10 competitors have.

   SeoQuake: PR: 6 | I: 55,700 | L: 37,124 | LD: 3,493,256 | I: 268000 | Rank: 5199 | Age: Mar 02, 2000

- **Link Quality**

   Why It's Important: Link quantity is important, but link quality is more important. You want links from high quality sites related to your site. One of my favorite tools to use is Open Site Explorer (http://www.opensiteexplorer.org).

How You Can Check this Metric: Use Open Site Explorer to find out who's linking to you and who's linking to your top 10 competitors.

What to Do About This: If your link profile is worse than your competitors (i.e. their links are earned based on merit and come from quality sites, and your links come from free directories, link farms and other low-quality link sources), you need to revert this trend. Learn from your competitors and emulate the good things they do.

- **Anchor Text**

  Why It's Important: When you try to rank for "sporting goods," a link like "check out our sporting goods" is much more valuable than "for sporting goods click here." You want your keywords in the anchor text of your links.

  How You Can Check this Metric: Use Open Site Explorer.

  What to Do About This: If most of your incoming links don't contain your keywords, start a link building campaign and get keyword-rich text links. Also, don't forget that internal links are very important. You have full control as to how you interlink pages within your site, so be smart and use keywords here.

- **PageRank (PR)**

  Why It's Important: The higher your PageRank, the more link juice you have to distribute to your pages and get them indexed and ranked high.

  How You Can Check this Metric: The SEOQuake toolbar can help you check this metric for your site and your top 10 competitors.

  SeoQuake: PR: 6 | I: 55,700 | L: 37,124 | LD: 3,493,256 | I: 268000 | Rank: 5199 | Age: Mar 02, 2000

  What to Do About This: If your competitors have a higher PageRank (PR) than your site, work on getting links. When external sites link to you, they pass PR to your site. Also, watch your PR distribution. Assign the no-follow attribute to links that point to pages you don't care about such as Terms of Use, Privacy Policy, etc.

- **Site Age**

  Why It's Important: The older your site, the higher your chances to rank at the top (especially on Google).

  How You Can Check this Metric: The SEOQuake toolbar can help you check this metric for your site and your top 10 competitors.

  SeoQuake: PR: 6 | I: 55,700 | L: 37,124 | LD: 3,493,256 | I: 268000 | Rank: 5199 | Age: Mar 02, 2000

  What to Do About This: You can always buy an older site, but you can't change how old your site is. Even if you can't do anything about it, it is important to check this metric. If the top 10 sites on Google are fifteen years old and your site is only one year old, you will have to work hard in other SEO areas to make up for being so "young."

- **AllInAnchor**

  Why It's Important: You need to know if your incoming links' anchor texts are optimized for your keywords.

  To search for keywords manually, type the following in Google's browser.

  AllinAnchor:keyword

  What to Do About This: If your AllInAnchor ranking for a given keyword is lower than your regular ranking for that keyword, work on getting links with your keyword as the anchor text.

- **AllInTitle**

  Why It's Important: You need to know if your page titles are optimized enough.

  To search for keywords manually, type the following in Google's browser.

  AllinTitle:keyword

  What to Do About This: If your AllInTitle ranking for a given keyword is lower than your regular ranking for that keyword, optimize your page title and add your keyword to it.

- **AllInText**

  Why It's Important: You need to know if your page content is optimized enough.

  To search for keywords manually, type the following in Google's browser.

  AllinText:keyword

  What to Do About This: If your AllInText ranking for a given keyword is lower than your regular ranking for that keyword, optimize your page content and add your keyword to it.

- **Duplicate Content**

  Why It's Important: Internal duplicate content can kill your rankings. Detect and eliminate it.

  How You Can Check this Metric: Use Open Site Explorer.

  What to Do About This: Write unique titles, meta descriptions and meta keywords tags for all pages.

- **Website Architecture Issues**

  Why It's Important: You need to make sure your website is built right and search engines can spider it.

  How You Can Check this Metric: Use SEO Browser (http://www.seobrowser.com) to see your site the way search engines see it. Make sure search engines can spider it and follow your links.

- **Keyword Cannibalization Issues**

  Why It's Important: When several pages on your site are competing for the same keywords, your rankings can suffer. Concentrate all this optimization on one page instead.

  How You Can Check this Metric: Do this Google search:

  Google will show you what pages of your site are the most relevant for a given keyword, and will sort them in order of relevance.

  What to Do About This: If you have several pages that are optimized for a keyword, pick one and from all the other pages, link to that one page using your keyword in the anchor text.

- **On-Site Optimization Score**

  Why It's Important: One of the best ways to rank high is to look at the 10 websites that rank at the top. Then find patterns among them and replicate them.

  How You Can Check this Metric: Although this can be done manually, it's a lot more effective to use a tool. I suggest using IBP (http://www.ibusinesspromoter.com) – one of my favorite tools.

What to Do About This: Run the Top 10 Report on IBP. The software will give you an on-page optimization score, and will tell you what to do to improve your score.

Step #3 On-Page Optimization

The third step in SEO is on-page optimization. Use this example to create a "perfectly" optimize page - from headline to images.

The "Perfectly" Optimized Page
(for the example keyword phrase "chocolate donuts")

Page Title: Chocolate Donuts | Mary's Bakery

Meta Description: Mary's Bakery's chocolate donuts are possibly the most delicious, perfectly formed, flawlessly chocolately donuts ever made.

H1 Headline:
Chocolate Donuts from Mary's Bakery

Image Filename: chocolate-donuts.jpg

Photo of Donuts (with Alt Attribute): Chocolate Donuts

Body Text: _____ chocolate donuts _____ donuts _____ chocolate donuts _____ donuts chocolate _____ chocolate donuts _____ chocolate _____ chocolate donuts

Page URL: http://marysbakery.com/chocolate-donuts

Image Source: http://www.seomoz.org/blog

Title Tags

- Each page of your site needs to have its own title.

- Use Google Webmaster Tools to find duplicate title tags on your site.

- Use your keyword at the beginning of your title tag. If your keyword is "back pain treatment," your page title could be "Back Pain Treatment - How to Treat Back Pain."

- Don't stuff your keyword several times in the title. Use the keyword once and then a variation of that keyword (see example above).

- Don't go over 66 characters.

- Google will show your page title in its search results, so make sure you write compelling page titles that attract clicks. This is a good listing optimized for the keyword "promotional items:"

Branded Promotional Items and Cool Gadgets - **Sunshine Products ...**
Looking for the Coolest Gadgets on the Internet or Promotional Items for Your Company? You Are in the Right Place. Check Out Out Bestsellers!
www.sunshineproductsusa.com/ - Cached - Similar

- Notice how the title grabs your attention. The meta description includes a call to action towards the end.

- The page title describes the content on the page. As a rule of thumb, if people can tell what your page is about from reading your page title and meta description, you are on the right track.

Meta Descriptions

- Put your keyword here - the main goal of the meta description is to attract clicks.

> **The Outsourcing Company** - Internet Marketing Agency
> Boost Your Website Traffic and Skyrocket Your Online Sales. Search Engine Optimization, Pay per Click and Social Media. FREE Initial Consultation!
> About Us - Blog - Search Engine Optimization - Web Design
> www.theoutsourcingcompany.com/ - Cached - Similar

- It also includes a strong call to action which invites people to click.

- Each page of your site needs to have its own meta description.

- Don't make your meta descriptions longer than 160 characters.

- Use Google Webmaster Tools to find duplicate meta descriptions on your site.

- When a visitor reads your meta description and can immediately tell what your page is about, then you have a good description.

Meta Keywords

- They are not as important as they used to be, and Google doesn't even consider them. However, Yahoo and MSN still pay attention to meta keywords. They can be written in seconds so it's definitely worth including them.

- Don't put your "money" keywords here, because this is the first place your competitors will look to steal your keywords.

- Make sure your meta keywords are related to the content of your page.

Body Text

- Include your keywords in the body text of your pages.

- Write for your visitors, and not for search engines. Don't stuff keywords throughout your pages, because it makes your text confusing and unreadable.

H Tags

- "H" stands for headline. H1 is the main headline and H2 is the sub-headline, etc. Use H tags and put your keywords in them.

URLs

- Each page should have its own URL.

- Use keyword-rich URLs.

- If you have a lot of content, organize it in folders. For example, www.site.com/shoes/adidas/arbolado-155PCX/.

- Don't use session IDs or any other variable that can generate different URLs for the same destination.

- If you need to change URLs, use 301 redirects.

HTML Header

A page header is the first part of an HTML document. A header should look like this:

<!DOCTYPE html PUBLIC "-//W3C//DTD XHTML 1.0 Transitional//EN">

<html>

<head>

<meta http-equiv="Content-Type" content="text/html; charset=UTF-8" />

<title>Travel Gadgets – The Coolest Travel Gadgets in the World</title>

<meta name="description" content="If You Are Looking for Travel Gadgets, STOP Looking! We Have the Largest Selection at Discounted Prices and FREE Shipping Worldwide. Shop Now!" />

<meta name="keywords" content="travel gadgets, affordable travel gadgets, cool travel gadgets" />

<meta name="robots" content="noodp,noydir" />

<meta name="author" content="Zeke Camusio" />

The robots meta tag is telling the search engines not to take your website description from DMOZ (http://www.dmoz.org/) or Yahoo! Directory (http://dir.yahoo.com/). The other lines are pretty self-explanatory.

Fix Canonical URL Issues

If you can access your site by typing "site.com" and "www.site.com," Google will see those as two different sites with the exact same content which can really hurt your SEO. Create a file called .htaccess with these three lines and put it in the root folder of your site:

RewriteEngine On

RewriteCond %{HTTP_HOST} !^www\.site\.com$

RewriteRule (.*) http://www.site.com/$1 [R=301,L]

Warning: Unless you know what you're doing, have someone else do this. All servers are configured different and you don't want to mess with your .htaccess file.

Landing Pages

After you've optimized your existing pages, it's time to create your landing pages.

- Create one landing page for each keyword.

- Optimize page titles, meta descriptions, meta keywords, body text, H tags and URLs for your landing pages.

- Link to your landing pages from several pages of your site. Put your keywords in the anchor texts. For example, if you link to www.site.com/tennis-rackets.html, make the links say tennis rackets.

- Use IBP to compare your landing pages with the top 10 ranking sites for your keywords. Make all necessary adjustments until you get an IBP score of 85% of higher.

Website Architecture and Usability

- Make sure your website is "SEO compliant."

- Use descriptive anchor texts - "tennis rackets" instead of "click here."

- Images should have ALT tags (this has more to do with accessibility issues than it does with SEO).

- Make sure your text isn't inside Flash animations or images so search engines can read it (use SEO Browser to check how Google sees your site).

- Avoid frames.

- Use DIVs instead of tables for layout.

- Make sure your content can be spidered (use SEO Browser and Google Webmaster Tools to check for spider crawlability issues).

- Organize your content. If you have over 20 pages, draw a map of all pages and how they link to each other. Group your content so search engines can easily understand your website. For example, if you have 200 Nike shoes and 200 Adidas shoes, don't put all 400 links on your home page. Have a link to "shoes" on your home page, links to "Adidas" on your "shoes" page and links to the Adidas shoes on the "Adidas" page. Segment your shoes by size, color or any criteria you want.

- Send PageRank to the pages you want to rank. Make your links to irrelevant pages "no-follow." Some irrelevant pages might be: privacy policy, terms of use, log in, shopping cart and external links to sites you don't want to send PageRank.

- Keep your code clean. Get rid of garbage code. Use external JavaScripts and CSS stylesheets to keep pages as light as possible.

- Run HTML Validator (http://validator.w3.org/) and fix big problems. Don't worry if you don't get a 100% valid page.

- Fix broken links with WC3 Link Checker (http://validator.w3.org/checklink/).

- Make sure there's a 404 error page and there aren't broken links on it. This is important - prevents search engine bots from looping around your site.

- Make sure there is a robots.txt file, and it doesn't stop search engines from crawling your site. Disallow sections of your website you don't want indexed such as: printer-friendly versions of your pages, your shopping cart, admin area, etc.

- Create an HTML Sitemap and an XML Sitemap with XML Sitemaps Generator (http://www.xml-sitemaps.com/)

- Make sure Google knows where your company is located. Enter an address in the website footer, have a proper TLD (.co.uk for the UK, .es for Spain, .com for the US, etc.), and choose your location from Google Webmaster Tools.

- Make sure Google Analytics (http://www.google.com/analytics/index.html) is installed and all goals are set up.

- Fix duplicate content issues:

  1. External duplicate content - the same content is posted on your site and other websites. This kind of duplicate content does not affect your rankings. If it did, your competitors

could easily get you penalized by making several copies of your site and putting them online.

2. Internal duplicate content - this could really hurt your site. Look for several versions of the same content.

3. Near-duplicate content - sometimes pages aren't completely identical but they have little unique content. For example, if you have an e-commerce website, most of your pages have some elements in common: navigation menu, footer, etc. If the only difference on your pages is a one sentence description, they might be considered duplicate content.

4. Do you have PDF versions of your pages?

5. Printer-friendly versions?

6. Do you have the same content on more than one page (such as the Home Page and About Us)?

7. Does http://yoursite.com automatically redirect to http://www.yoursite.com? It should.

8. Do you have absolute links (http://www.yoursite.com/page1.html) instead of relative links (page1.html)? You should.

9. Do you link to your home page http://www.yoursite.com/ instead of http://www.yoursite.com/index.html? You should.

10. Duplicate tags - this is the most dangerous duplicate content. When all page titles and descriptions are the same across your entire website, Google doesn't like you. Use Google Webmaster Tools to detect duplicate tags and correct them immediately.

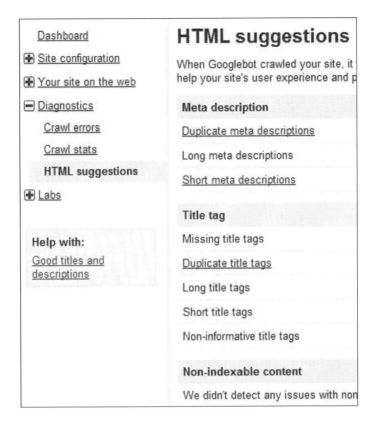

- Make sure your page is indexed - Google ranks pages, not sites. Take the page you want to rank for a given keyword and run a Google search:

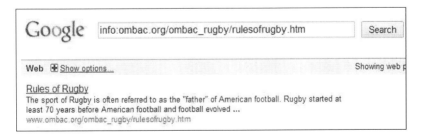

- Check Google's cache to make sure your page has been indexed recently.

 cache:ombac.org/ombac_rugby/rulesofrugby.htm

It is a snapshot of the page as it appeared on 28 Dec 2009 02:48:28 GMT.

How to Optimize Your Blog

I highly recommend WordPress (www.WordPress.org) for your blog. Once your blog is installed on your site, use the following plug-ins to optimize it.

- **Permalinks**
  Permalinks are URLs of your individual blog posts. Go to WordPress, choose "Settings" and then go into "Permalinks" and check "Custom, specify below" and customize your permalinks **/%category%/%postname%/** (this is the perfect permalink). If you don't have different categories, just use the post name.

- **All In One SEO Pack**
  (http://wordpress.org/extend/plugins/all-in-one-seo-pack/) Allows you to optimize WordPress blogs – customizes meta tags, descriptions, titles, etc.

- **Google XML Sitemaps**
  (http://wordpress.org/extend/plugins/google-sitemap-generator) Generates XML sitemap which helps search engines index your blog better.

- **Target Blank in Posts and Comments**
  (http://wordpress.org/extend/plugins/target-blank-in-

posts-and-comments/) When visitors click on external links within your blog, it opens a new window but still keeps visitors on your blog.

- **Automatic SEO Links** (http://wordpress.org/extend/plugins/automatic-seo-links/) If you forget to manually include links, just choose a URL or word and it will replace matches in your blog posts.

- **SEO Friendly Images** (http://wordpress.org/extend/plugins/seo-image/) Automatically adds title and alt attributes to images within blog post (improves search engine traffic).

- **PubSubHubbub** (http://wordpress.org/extend/plugins/pubsubhubbub/)Visi tors are informed in "real-time" when you update your blog.

How to "Localize" SEO with Google SERP

Important Note: Watch this Webinar on Local SEO: http://www.theoutsourcingcompany.com/blog/internet-marketing-events/free-webinar-seo-for-local-businesses/

Google claims that over 20 percent of all their searches are for local businesses, places, etc. With the changes Google has made to their SERPs, they clearly favor local search results.

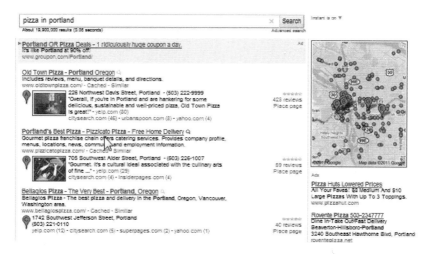

Google Place (http://places.google.com/business) pages now appear like full search results with the Map moved to the far right. When Google determines the search term is definitely local, Place pages will dominate the results often appearing above organic results (i.e. Pizza in Portland). When the term is likely local, the Pack 7 will appear among the results (i.e. pizza).

With Google placing their Place pages among organic results (and in many cases, above organic results), your Place page ranking becomes more important than ever. To improve your ranking:

- Optimize your Google Places page

- Optimize your website and landing pages for local searches

- Leverage citations

- Get more customer reviews

How to Optimize Your Google Places Page

- **Claim Your Google Place Page**

  Google may have already generated a Place page for you. Just claiming your Place page helps improve your rank. If you plan to do optimization to outrank your competitors, you can't begin without first claiming your page.

- **Set Up Service Area**

  If you are a plumber that services Seattle, Bellevue and Redmond but your business address is Redmond, you will not appear in searches for a "plumber in Seattle" or "plumber in Bellevue." You will need to go into your Places page and select "Yes, this business serves customers at their locations," and then define your service area to include Seattle, Bellevue and Redmond.

- **Verify Address is Correct**

  This has as much to do with customer service as it has to do with SEO. If you have a physical address such as a restaurant or store, make sure Google Places has the address listed correctly. Do not use a PO Box.

- **Always Show Your Address**

  Google Places gives you the option to hide your address. DO NOT hide your address! Hiding your address negatively impacts your ranking (even for service areas).

- **Choose the Right Categories**

  Conduct market research and find out the most commonly used business categories associated with your business. You can check out your competitors' Place pages and Superpages for category ideas. Make sure to use at least one of Google's default categories.

- **Use Keywords in Place Page Description**

  Although you shouldn't stuff your description with keywords, a complete description using keywords will help your ranking.

- **Add Photos and Video to Page**

  By including photos and/or video on your Place Page, you contribute to your page's completeness and improve your ranking. Photos and videos also help your page stand out among search results. When you make your page more useful to customers, you improve both your click-through-rate and conversion rate.

- **List Phone Number with Local Area Code**

  When you list your phone number on your page, make sure it includes the same area code as your target market. If you don't have a local number, get a free number using a service such as Google Voice (http://www.google.com/voice). You can set it up so that when a customer calls your new local number, it will direct the call to the phone you currently use.

- **What to Avoid:**

o Multiple Places Pages with the same phone number

o Multiple Places Pages with the same address (if you rent office space with many businesses in the same building, be sure to include your suite number).

o Hiding your address

o Never use an 800 number

- **How to Optimize Your Linked Website and Landing Pages for Google Places**

o A company website helps your Places Page ranking by adding to your company's credibility. The links you list on your Places Page should point to area-specific landing pages, which only contain information for a specific area (i.e. Link To Portland Landing Page, Link to Oregon City Landing Page).

o Include city and state in all website title tags. This will help both your organic and local rankings.

o Include your full address on your landing pages. Make sure your address is formatted correctly by typing it into Google Maps (http://maps.google.com/).

o Include your local area code phone number on your landing pages.

o Include the location keyword in the anchor text of inbound links like this: plumber in Portland o The URL's should contain the location keyword: http://mycompany.com/Portland-Plumbing

o If you have multiple locations, create separate landing pages for each location.

- **What to Avoid:**

o Never list a PO Box on your website without including your physical address.

o Never include 800 numbers. If you have an 800 number listed on your website and don't include local numbers, it can lower your ranking.

- **Leveraging Citations**

  Being listed on third-party sites like Superpages, Yelp, Citysearch, etc. helps to establish your credibility which improves your ranking. These are the most important factors that affect your page ranking:

  o **Consistency** – Make sure your business name, address and phone number are the same for all directories and exactly matches the information on Google Places.

  o **Quantity of Citations** – The more directories you're listed in, the better.

  o **Quality of Citations** – Being listed in directories of well-known and trusted directories gives your page ranking a boost (as well as being listed in local directories).

- o **Top 10 Citation Sites -** Note: List is via local search engine ranking factors

  - Superpages (http://www.superpages.com/)

  - infoUSA (http://www.infousa.com/)

  - Yellowpages/CanPages (http://www.yellowpages.com/) (http://www.canpages.ca/)

  - Niche Industry Sites (i.e. http://www.urbanspoon.com/)

  - Citysearch (http://www.citysearch.com/)

  - Localeze (http://www.localeze.com/)

  - Yelp (http://www.yelp.com/)

  - Yahoo (http://dir.yahoo.com/)

  - Acxiom (http://www.acxiom.com/)

  - InsiderPages (http://www.insiderpages.com/)

Additional sites:

- Municipal Sites (Chamber of Commerce, Local Directories)

- Kudzu (http://www.kudzu.com/)

- DexKnows (http://www.dexknows.com/)

- Angie's List (http://www.angieslist.com/)

- Merchant Circle (http://www.merchantcircle.com/)

Customer Reviews

Although Google has stated that positive (or negative) reviews do not affect Place page ranking, other review factors can impact your rank.

- **Volume of Reviews** – The impact that volume will have on your ranking depends on the review volume of your competition. Try to have at least as many customer reviews as your competition.

- **Velocity of Reviews** – If you get a ton of reviews all at once, it will look "spammy" to Google and you may get penalized. Ideally, you want a consistent stream of reviews.

- **Reviews Left Directly On Google** – Reviews left by Google accounts with a long account history are more likely to be trusted by Google (compared to people who sign up for a Google account prior to writing a review).

- **Location and Product Keywords in Reviews** – You don't have direct control over what your customers write, but you can suggest they mention your location and product/service when they write online reviews. When it comes to customer reviews, being passive won't cut it. Reach out to customers you've recently sold to and ask for their feedback. Offer your existing customers a discount on future purchases as a way to thank them for their review.

Step #4 Content Creation

Good content is another key to your SEO success. Use these six tips to improve your content.

Tip #1: Don't Stuff Keywords

Stuffing keywords looks awful and your readers won't appreciate it. It is okay to put your keywords wherever they makes sense, but don't overdo it. Your goal is to get buyers and not just visitors. You will repel visitors if all they see is a flood of keywords on your site.

Tip #2: Give Too Much Away for FREE

Everybody is putting out good information these days. However, "good" isn't good enough anymore. You have to go the extra mile and reveal all your secrets. The good news is that most people will see your content and think: "This is great! She really knows what she's talking about. But this is too much work and I don't want to do it myself. I'll hire her to do it for me." Don't be afraid of people "stealing" your secrets. If you don't reveal them, your competitors will.

Tip #3: Make Complex Things Simple

Nothing is new and everything has been written already. The problem is that most people are lousy communicators and write confusing, boring content. Take complex information and lay it out in a simple "step-by-step" way that readers can easily understand.

Tip #4: Be Yourself

Most people who find writing difficult are trying to be someone else. Just be yourself, and write like you talk. People appreciate original personalities.

Tip #5: Have Two-Way Conversations

Ask for feedback and comments. Ask questions. It should not be about you - it should be about your readers. Get your audience involved and they will feel part of something bigger.

Tip #6: Seven Proven Types of Content

I have tested a variety of content, and these are seven types that proved to work over and over again.

- "How To" articles (How to Read Faster, How to Save $100 per Week, etc.)

- Lists (7 Secrets, 5 Ways, Top 10, etc.)

- Demos and tutorials (don't tell them how it's done, SHOW them)

- Step-by-step guides

- Case studies (people love reading about others just like them who made it big)

- Expert interviews

- News (tie current events to what's happening in your industry)

Market Research

These are great tools to use for your content market research.

Google Keyword Tool

Step 1: Find Long-Tail Keywords

If you want to write an article about growing tomatoes, you obviously want to include the keywords "grow tomatoes" and "growing tomatoes" in your article. What about less obvious keywords? Use the Google Keyword Tool to find more suggestions.

Keywords
Keywords related to term(s) entered
growing tomatoes
grow tomatoes
tomato growing
how to grow tomatoes
grow tomato
how to grow tomato
grow tomato plants
growing tomato plants
growing tomatoes pots
growing tomatoes from seed
growing tomatoes in pots
growing tomatos
tomato growing tips
tomatos growing
grow tomatos
growing tomatoes upside down
grow tomato plant
growing tomatoes containers

Step 2: Put Several of These Keywords in Your Content

Some of these keywords are somewhat competitive, and you will never rank for them unless you optimize your website more, create more content around them and build anchor text links. But some of these keywords are extremely easy to rank for, and just by placing the keyword in your content you can rank on the first page of Google for that keyword.

The better your content is and the more you promote it, the more links you will get. More links help you rank higher – and the more you promote your content, the better you will rank for all keywords you included.

Forums

A great way to research your content is to go straight to the source - research online forums. Find out what topics people are talking about on discussions boards. For example, if you wanted to find topics about "Internet marketing" conduct a Google search for "Internet marketing discussion boards."

As you check out the boards and forums, sort discussion threads by views and find out what threads have the most replies and views. If large groups of people are interested in certain topics (i.e. how to rank high in Google), they will probably be interested in reading content about that topic.

Ask Your Audience

Ask your Twitter and Facebook followers what topics interest them. This is a quick and easy way to find out what's on your audience's mind.

Step #5 Link Building

Link building is another important SEO step. You want websites to link back to your site, and remember you don't want just any random link out there. Be strategic with your link building.

Rule #1: The More, The Merrier
You want as many links as possible.

Rule #2: Links from Authoritative Sites Are More Valuable
A link from CNN.com is worth more than a link from your cousin's blog. Look for sites that have a Domain Authority (DA) of 55 or more. You can use the SEOMoz Toolbar (http://www.seomoz.org/seo-toolbar) to view the DA of a site.

Rule #3: Topical Relationship Matters
If you own a dog training website, a link from another dog training website is more valuable than a link from a music e-store.

Rule #4: The Page the Link Is Pointing to Matters
Don't forget that search engines rank pages, not domains. Try to get links that point to the pages you want to rank. This is better than getting links that point only to your home page.

Rule #5: Link Text is Everything
If I want to rank at the top of Google for "Internet Marketing Agency," the link <u>Internet Marketing Agency</u> is more valuable than <u>Click Here</u>. In fact, I'd rather get 10 links with my keyword in them than 100 links with irrelevant link text. When two or more links point to the same URL, it is the first link in the HTML code that counts.

Rule #6: Context Matters
The text surrounding a link matters, and so does the location of the link on a page. A text link in the first paragraph is worth more than a tiny link buried in the page footer.

Rule #7: Internal Links Count
I'm always shocked at how many people use "click here" or "read more" to link to other pages within their sites. You have full control over your website, so why not make those links keyword-rich? Use Xenu's Link Sleuth (<u>http://home.snafu.de/tilman/xenulink.html</u>) to check for broken internal links:

Rule #8: Not All Links Last Forever
Use Link Atrophy Diagnosis (<u>http://www.virante.com/seo-tools/link-atrophy-diagnosis-tool.php</u>) to measure how long your links last.

Rule #9: Make It Look Natural

Dozens of new links built overnight pointing to the same page and using the perfect anchor text does not look natural. Mix it up. Link to the home page sometimes, use anchor texts like "click here" or www.site.com, and make sure you don't build too many links too fast.

Rule #10: Beware of NoFollow Links

"NoFollow" links do not count. Find out more on Wikipedia (http://en.wikipedia.org/wiki/Nofollow). Use the SEOMoz Toolbar to detect nofollow links.

Three Different Ways to Get Links

1. **Earn Them** – When you have great content, people will automatically link to your site even when you don't ask them. This is the most effective way to build links.

2. **Build Them** – Add links to forums, blogs, directories, etc.

3. **Ask for Them** – Contact webmasters and bloggers, and ask them to link to your site.

Link Building Tactics

From Sites that Link to Your Competitors

Use the SEOMoz Link Intersect Tool (http://www.seomoz.org/) to find out who's linking to the five sites that are ranking first on Google for your keywords.

SEOMoz is a paid tool so use the following as a free alternative. Type the following search modifer into Google: **linkdomain:mbjessee.com -site:mbjessee.com** This allows you to see who is linking to your competitors on Google.

Get links from these sites:

- If the site is a blog, offer a guest post.

- If the site is a forum, post an article.

- If the site has a Resources/Links section, try to get listed here.

- If the site is a directory or allows for websites to get listed on it, submit your link.

- If you find broken links on websites, use this as a conversation opener when you contact the webmasters. When they reply, offer them content. If they don't have broken links, make a suggestion or give them a compliment on their site. Use the telephone, email and social networks to contact these webmasters. Use a CRM tool to follow up with them because starting a conversation by asking for a link isn't very effective. Use common sense and relationship skills to understand what webmasters and their visitors want. Once you know what they want, you can give it to them.

From Top Ranking Sites

Find top ranking sites for given keywords and get links from them using the same principles explained in the previous tactic.

Advanced Article Marketing

1. Submit articles to EzineArticles (http://www.ezinearticles.com)

2. Track a unique snippet of each article using Google Alert (http://www.google.com/alerts).

3. When you receive an alert indicating that someone posted one of your articles on their site, look at their site. If the site looks good (relevant or high PageRank, high traffic volume and Alexa Rank, and many comments/retweets), offer them more content (maybe exclusive content).

4. The goal is always to control the anchor text on the links in articles.

Directories - Refer to Appendix: Tools (Chapter 3)

Guest Blogging

The most influential bloggers in your industry have access to thousands of people you don't. When your content gets published on their blogs, you automatically gain access to all these people. The most influential bloggers in your industry are seen as highly trusted experts in their field. If these bloggers trust you, so will their readers.

1. Do a Google search for [keyword] blog.

2. Check the top 50 results and find blogs with a high volume of followers/readers. The best way to find out if a blog gets high traffic is by checking the comments on their blog posts. Active, high traffic blogs receive many comments.

Posted in: Gardening, Troubleshooting | 11 Comments »

3. Subscribe to the blogs and comment often. Bloggers love it when people comment on their blogs.

4. Once they get to know you, send bloggers emails and congratulate them on their blogs. Don't ask for anything yet. Just say something nice.

5. Keep building these relationships. There's no magic number as to how many emails to send them. Just play it by ear. Find ways to help them. If you have suggestions for ways to improve their sites or topics, send them your feedback.

6. Once you have a great relationship with bloggers, tell them you have a great idea for an article and ask them if they'd like to publish it. Don't ask for a "guest blogging position" - ask for a small commitment instead (one article on a great topic!) Tell them that you will write it. If they read it and decide not to publish it, let the blogger know you won't be offended.

7. After your first article is published, ask you friends to check it out and comment on it. Most bloggers love comments and the more they get, the happier they will be.

8. At this point, go for a slightly bigger commitment (two articles per month or one per week).

9. Build real relationships with bloggers. Don't just kiss their butt to get something from them. This won't take you very far.

10. This is a great guest blogging resource: http://www.myblogguest.com/. Don't forget to translate your blog into other languages.

Link Building Search Engine Queries

Use these search engine queries to look for sites to place links:

- [mdkw] inurl:category/guest

- [mdkw] "guest blogger"

- [mdkw] guest blog post writer

- [mdkw] "guest post"

- [mdkw] "guest article"

- [mdkw] "guest column"

- [mdkw] inurl:contributors

- {keyword} "guest blogger" OR "guest post" OR "guest article" OR "guest column"

- {keyword} "become a contributor" OR "contribute to this site"

- {keyword} "write for us" OR "write for me"

- {keyword} inurl:category/guest

- {keyword} "top * [tools/ articles/ websites/ etc.]" -> refine search to ~1 year ago. Contact anybody who shows up and ask if you can help with the 2009/ 20** edition of the article

- [pr welcome], [submit * review], [pr friendly], [pr contact], [pr info], [get * reviewed], [allintitle:get * reviewed], [reviews inurl:submit]

- [intitle:submit intitle:contest], [allintitle:submit * contest], [blog contests], [submit * giveaway]

- ["in kind donations" list], ["in kind donors" list]

- intitle:[{target keyword} videos], intitle:[{target keyword} clips]

- intitle:[{target keyword} tools], intitle:[free {target keyword} tools], intitle:[list of free {target keyword} tools], intitle:[list of {target keyword} tools]

- "keyword phrase" sponsor charity

- "public library" "useful links" keyword phrase site:.gov

- "useful keyword phrase sites" library –clientwebsite site:.edu

- "helpful keyword phrase sites" library –clientwebsite site:.edu

- "favorite keyword phrase sites" library –clientwebsite site:.edu

- "best keyword phrase" site:.edu OR site:.org

- keyword phrase resources public library site:.us

- keyword phrase site:.edu

- In Google Image Search to find the little "U Comment – I Follow" logo: "MY KEYPHRASE" inurl:ifollow*.gif

- [mdkw] blog list

- [mdkw] top bloggers

- [mdkw] blogroll

- [mdkw] "blog roll"

- [mdkw] twitter list

- [mdkw] twitter users

- [mdkw] "list of lists"

- [mdkw] "top * ways"

- [mdkw] "top * tips"

- [mdkw] "top 10"

- [mdkw] "top 100"

- [mdkw] intitle:"q/a with"

- [mdkw] intitle:"q&a with"

- [mdkw] intitle:experts interview OR talk OR discuss OR answer

- [mdkw] expert interview

- [mdkw] intitle:interview

- ["Notify me of follow-up comments?"+"Submit the word you see below:"]

Ontolo Tool

Use this tool to get an additional list of sites to place links.
http://link-building-tools.ontolo.com/LinkBuildingQueries.php

Open Site Explorer Tool

Check your competitors' links and sort the results by page authority.
http://www.opensiteexplorer.org/

SEOMoz Tool (subscription fee)

If you are serious about SEO, this is a really good tool to use.
http://www.seomoz.org/labs/link-finder/index.php

Juicy Link Finder (subscription fee)

http://www.seomoz.org/link-finder/

Business Partners

Ask your vendors, business partners, friends and people you know to link to you.

Events and Charities (PR Coverage)

Organize several events, and make sure bloggers know about and write about your events.

Awards

Give an award and give the winners a badge to put on their site (which will link to you, using the image CSS replacement technique so you can take full advantage of the link text).

Testimonials

Offer testimonials every time you buy something online - as long as they allow you to put a link to your site in the testimonial.

Donations and Sponsorships

Make a donation and ask them to put your site on the Supporters' page. Become a sponsor and ask them to link to your site.

Get More Links from Previous Linkers

Keep a list of all sites that linked to you in the past, and send them more content so they continue linking to you.

Content Distribution

Every time you have a new article, post it to Ping.fm, OnlyWire, EzineArticles, forums, Facebook, Twitter and LinkedIn. Include a call to action inviting people to re-post those articles to their sites and link back to you.

Blog Commenting

Post relevant comments to blogs in your industry.

Contests and Badges

Organize crazy contests to get people to talk about you. Give winners badges to put on their sites so they link back to your site (as mentioned above with awards).

"Link to This"

Have this call to action all over your website. Give people the HTML code of whatever they want to link to so it's easier for them to link to your site. By asking them to "link this," it allows more people to take direct action.

Create the Updated Version of an Old Resource

Search for content such as "10 places to visit in 2006" and then write the 2011 version. Find out who is linking to the 2006 version, and tell them you have a more updated version of the article (so they will link to the updated version).

Look for Broken Links and Replace Them with Your Resources

If you have a travel site, search for Travel Resources. You will find many sites that list their favorite travel resources. Use this Firefox add-on http://www.kevinfreitas.net/extensions/linkchecker/ to highlight broken links on these resource pages. Contact the webmasters and let them know about the broken links. Suggest that they put your site there to replace the broken link.

Find other sites linking to that same resource, and get those people to link to you instead (because your resource works and it's not a broken link).

How to find these resources:

- Your subject + [Calculator/Lifehack/Tip/Resource/List]

- Search on Delicious (http://www.delicious.com/) and run their broken link tool.

- DMOZ/Yahoo/Niche directories

- Get a list of the sites on pages 5-20 of Google. Run them by Open Site Explorer. Click on Top Pages and look for 404 errors. Find sites linking to these pages and get them to link to you instead of a broken link.

Tools

Create plenty of innovative tools and fun quizzes. People will link to these tools. Also, give people badges to put on their sites.

Viral Campaigns

Create a diverse linkbait content such as lists, reports, tools, games, etc. This book gives more helpful ideas:
http://www.amazon.com/Outrageous-Advertising-Thats-Outrageously-Successful/dp/0982379307/ref=pd_bxgy_b_img_a

Interview Experts in Your Industry or Just Talk About Them

Play to experts' egos. They will more than likely link to an article that's written about them.

Additional Link Building Tips

- Webmasters get tons of emails every day. Be different and use the phone!

- This is a great book that will assist you with your sales pitch http://www.amazon.com/Sales-Advantage-Keep-Sell-More/dp/0743215915 (after all, asking someone to link to you is selling.)

- When link requests come from a woman, they work better. Use this piece of information to your advantage.

- Don't put the title of "SEO Specialist" in your email signature. PR works a lot better.

- Make sure you send emails from the same domain you're requesting links. If you are an agency, ask your client to create an email account for you. Don't use a Gmail, Hotmail or Yahoo address.

Step #6. Analytics

Important Note: Watch this Webinar on Google Analytics: http://www.theoutsourcingcompany.com/blog/internet-marketing/all-you-need-to-know-about-google-analytics/

The last step in SEO is analytics – how you measure and analyze your SEO results. I recommend using Google Analytics and the Google Keyword Tool for your SEO analysis. Refer to Chapter 7 for more information about analytics.

Ten Minute SEO Checklist

Take ten minutes to review the six SEO steps. How can you improve your SEO? Where do you fall short?

1. **Keyword Research**

   - Are you using both long-tail and broad keywords?
   - Have you analyzed keywords for search volume, relevancy, ranking and difficulty?

2. **Competitive Analysis**

   - Are you using Google Webmaster Tools to check your metrics?
   - Are you using Open Site Explorer to check link quality, PageRank, anchor text, etc.?

3. **On-Page Optimization**

   - Are your title tags, headlines and meta descriptions optimized?
   - Are you using WordPress plug-ins to optimize your blog?

4. **Content Creation**

   - Are you using the Google Keyword Tool for keyword research?
   - Have you asked social media followers and browsed discussion boards for content ideas?

5. **Link Building**

   - Are quality websites linking back to your site?
   - Are you adding your links to directories?

6. **Analytics**

   - Are you using Google Analytics and Google Keyword Tool to measure your SEO results?

CHAPTER 4

HOW TO MANAGE AND OPTIMIZE PAY PER CLICK (PPC) CAMPAIGNS

Three Ways to Find Inexpensive PPC Traffic

Pay Per Click (PPC) is used on sites where advertisers only pay their hosts when their ads are clicked. It's typical for advertisers to bid on keywords based on their target audiences.

However, PPC campaigns can quickly become an expensive endeavor. As more advertisers leave TV, radio, billboards in favor of web advertising, the competition for each click continues to increase as does the cost. Sometimes each click can cost up to $5. That's very expensive traffic unless you're selling cancer treatments or legal services.

Bid on Competitor's URLs
You would be amazed at how many people type "YouTube.com" into a search engine instead of into the address bar. Each time someone types a competitor's website address into Google, there is an opportunity for you to show a very inexpensive ad to that consumer. You make that ad even more compelling by advertising,

as an alternative, to that competitor with their name in the ad copy. Sometimes these very targeted clicks will only cost you $0.05 per click.

Bid on Competitor's Names
It is the same idea as the URL, but you use the competitor's name instead. Traffic from clicks like this can be inexpensive and very targeted if you pick the right competitors.

Bid on Misspelled Words
You show inexpensive ads to people who accidently fat-fingered their keyboard or mistype the name. An ad like this could cost a fraction of the correctly spelled word. Use Spelling Typo Generator (http://tools.seobook.com/spelling/keywords-typos.cgi) to help find typos associated with important keywords.

Test Your Site with Cheap PPC
Inexpensive tactics to drive traffic to your site are a great way to fine tune your product price points, try out new guarantees, and experiment with special offers before you even sell products. The goal is to drive a lot of traffic and see what offers are the most useful. With traffic like this at less than $0.10 per click, you learn a lot about what works on your site and what needs to be changed. PPC can be expensive over time, but use tricks like these to experiment for a few dollars.

How to Reduce PPC Costs by 42 Percent...in Just 25 Minutes

Over the years, I have helped clients reduce their PPC costs, but I always considered it to be part of my "secret sauce" and didn't want to tell anyone. Don't get me wrong. There's nothing "secretive" about this trick. In fact, it's something that Google recommends. But here's the catch - nobody actually uses it. This trick alone has helped my company cut PPC costs by 42 percent for clients that managed their own campaigns or had campaigns managed by a rookie.

Here's my secret: this "trick" involves using negative keywords. Negative keywords are words that, when typed, will stop your ads from displaying. The most common one is "free." If you sell Metallica DVDs, by using "free" as a negative keyword you can stop your ad from showing when people search for "free Metallica DVDs."

How do you create the perfect list of negative keywords?

1. Use Google Keyword Tool
Search for your keywords using the Google Keyword Tool and spot possible negative keywords. For example, if you offer luxury rentals in Panama use the following words in your negative keyword bucket:

Keyword		Volume
panama beach condo rentals		Not enough data
panama vacation rental		4,400
panama beach vacation rentals		Not enough data
panama beach (florida) rentals		Not enough data
(car) rentals panama		3,600
panama beach house rentals		Not enough data
panama house rentals		Not enough data
panama rental property		880
beach rentals in panama		Not enough data
vacation rentals in panama		1,600
house rental panama		Not enough data
beach house rental panama		Not enough data
(long term) rentals panama		Not enough data
panama (florida) vacation rentals		Not enough data
panama rental (cars)		Not enough data
panama home rentals		Not enough data
panama rental homes		Not enough data
apartment rental panama		720
panama apartment rentals		720
panama rental houses		Not enough data
(car) ental in panama		720
house rentals in panama		Not enough data
panama (boat) rentals		Not enough data
(boat) ental panama		Not enough data

Your properties are in Panama, Central America, not Panama Florida, so put "Florida" as a negative keyword. You don't rent boats or cars, so add "car," "cars," "automobile," "automobiles," "truck," "boat" and everything else that can't be rented to your negative keywords list.

If you only offer short-term rentals, add "long" to the list. This is just the first screen of keyword suggestions. You can finds thousands of negative keywords if you keep scrolling down and search for variations of your main keyword.

You might think: "if someone wants to rent a boat and they see an ad for property rentals, why would they click on it anyway?" The answer - most people click first and read second. And that costs you money.

2. Use Google AdWords Reports

From your AdWords account go to Reporting > Create Report. Choose the Query Performance Report:

Select the date range and choose to see the keywords for all your campaign. This report will show you actual search terms people use to find you.

Most advertisers use broad match, which means they trust Google to decide if a search query is relevant to one of their keywords. "Panama plane rentals" and "Panama rentals" are definitely close terms, and if people search for the former and you have the latter on your keywords list, your ad might show.

By looking at the report you created from Google AdWords, you can see the actual search terms that trigger your ads and put the budget-killing words on the negative keywords list. You can also use WordTracker Free Keyword Tool (http://freekeywords.wordtracker.com) to find more negative keywords.

When trying this out for the first time, it might take two hours instead of 25 minutes, but I promise you that they will be your two most profitable hours ever.

No-Fail PPC System That Won't Cost You Thousands

This is the "no-fail" system I use to get millions of qualified visitors for just mere pennies.

Keyword Research

1. Use the **Google Keyword Tool** to get keyword suggestions for your site.

- Run the same tool on your competitors' websites.

- Use the same tool for "Descriptive words or phrases" as opposed to the "Website content" feature.

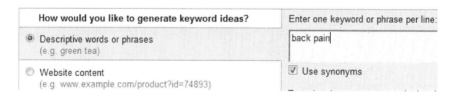

2. Use Word Tracker to get more keyword ideas.

3. Use SpyFu (http://www.spyfu.com/) to find out what keywords your competitors are using and get ideas from their campaigns. Looks for the 800 pound gorilla in your market and run SpyFu on their domain. They're very likely to have a huge budget and a well-optimized campaign. Let them do all the research, spend the money and learn from them.

4. Get synonyms from Synonyms (http://www.synonyms.com), Thesaurus (http://www.thesaurus.com) and Quintura (http://www.quintura.com).

5. Get misspellings using Spelling Typo Generator (http://tools.seobook.com/spelling/keywords-typos.cgi) Almost nobody bids on misspellings so you can find inexpensive clicks.

6. Bid on competitors' URLs. They are dirt cheap and extremely relevant. A lot of people do a Google search for YouTube.com instead of typing www.youtube.com into the address bar.

7. Another way to get cheap clicks is by having geo-targeted keywords such as "Seattle chiropractor." Make sure that you only bid on the keywords for the areas you serve and that landing pages contain those keywords. Otherwise, Google might think you are not relevant which hurts your Quality Score.

8. Bid on action keywords such as: "FIND local chiropractor" and "BUY PlayStation 3."

Consider the buying cycle. "Costa Rica beach condos" will get you less traffic than "Costa Rica," but it will be more qualified if you rent beach condos. Because you pay for each click, you only want qualified traffic.

Consider "side searches." Side searches are needs that you can fulfill but so can other products or services. For example, if you have beach condos in Costa Rica, you might want to bid for "honeymoon destinations."

SEO professionals recommend starting with thousands of keywords, but I don't recommend it. It's not a good idea because when a campaign is too big, it becomes too difficult to manage it. Start small. Ten percent of your keywords will drive 90 percent of your traffic.

Keyword Research for the Content Network

1. Bid on thought strings. If you sell weight loss pills, try strings like "[brand] didn't work for me," "has anyone tried [brand]?" etc. Look for things people would say in forums, blogs and discussion boards.

2. Bid on popular article titles. If there's a very popular article named "The 4-Minute Formula to Lose Weight Eating Chocolate," bid for it. Your ad will be displayed every time the article gets syndicated on a site running AdSense.

3. Do the same thing with book titles.

Campaign Structure and Settings

1. Have separate campaigns for search and content networks.

2. Have separate campaigns for broad and long-tail keywords. You'll want to pay less for broad keywords.

3. Use the Google AdWords Tracking code to track your campaign performance.

4. Choose to show your ads more evenly so it's easier to split-test them:

Advanced Options	
Keyword Bidding:	Maximum CPC bidding View and edit bidding options
Ad scheduling:	☐ Run at select times only ⑦ Running time: 72% of week Edit times and bids
Position preference:	☐ Enable position preferences ⑦
Ad serving: ⑦	○ Optimize: Show better-performing ads more often ◉ Rotate: Show ads more evenly

5. Choose the right geo-location for your campaign. This might sound obvious but you'd be surprised at how many people ship products to the U.S. only, but advertise across the world. If you are a chiropractor who serves the Seattle area, have two campaigns: one targeted to Seattle with keywords like "chiropractor" and "pain treatment, and another one targeted to the entire world with keywords like "Seattle chiropractor" and "pain treatment in Seattle."

6. Choose "Accelerated ad delivery." The Standard option spreads out your ads throughout the day. That's not good because when prospects search for your ads, they might not be there. By choosing Accelerated Ad Delivery, your ads will show every time until you hit your daily budget. That way you know when you need to increase your budget.

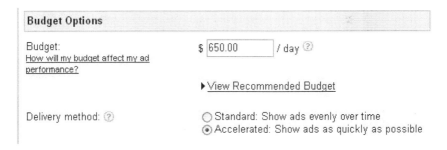

7. If you know that most people will buy your product between 10am and 5pm on week days, use ad scheduling.

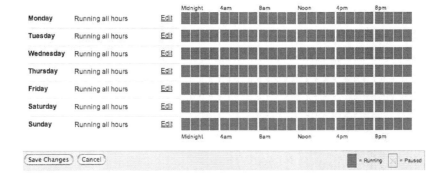

8. I set my budgets as high as possible. If a campaign makes me more than one dollar for every dollar invested, I want to invest as much money as Google is willing to take from me. If my campaign does not make money, then I just kill it. There's no reason to limit a campaign that is printing you money. Only limit your budget at the beginning when you test the campaign.

9. The best way to figure out how much you should start bidding is by using the Google Traffic Estimator Tool (https://adwords.google.com/o/Targeting/Explorer?__u=1000000000&__c=1000000000&ideaRequestType=KEYWORD_STATS#search.none). Enter different amounts and see how much traffic you get for each amount. Run your numbers and figure out what the perfect bid is. If you pay more than "the perfect bid," you will pay too much and you won't make a profit. If you pay less than "the perfect bid," you'll be leaving a lot of profitable traffic on the table. There's a sweet spot in between and Google's tool will help you find it.

10. Bids should end in 2 and 7 ($0.12, $0.17, $0.22), etc.

11. There are two factors that determine how much you'll pay for each click: your maximum bid and the Quality Score (QS). The QS is a grade that Google gives to your keywords based on how relevant your ads and landing pages are to that keyword. The higher your QS, the lower your cost per click. Include your keywords in your ads. The best way to do this is to group your keywords into ad groups and write one ad for each ad group.

12. Ideally, you should have one keyword per ad group but this is very time consuming. If you have a lot of time, go ahead and do it. If you don't, SpeedPPC (http://www.speedppc.com/) can do it for you. All the pros use tools like SpeedPPC, but if you're on a budget you can do it manually the first time. If you don't have the time or money, you don't absolutely need one ad for each keyword, but try to put your keywords in groups as small as possible. Don't just throw all your keywords into one ad group.

13. Put three match variations of each keyword into each ad group. For example, in the ad group "Costa Rica Vacations" you want to have the keywords "costa rica vacations" (use quotes for phrase match), [costa rica vacations] (use brackets for exact match) and costa rica vacations (don't use any special characters for broad match).

How to Create Successful PPC Ads

1. Include your keywords in your ads (on every line if possible) for higher QS and lower cost per click.

2. Use your headline to grab attention, the first line to mention the top benefits of your products and the third line for a clear call to action. You can use the URL line to include keywords and calls to action as well.

Webinar Software
Fast and Reliable Webinar Software.
Start Your FREE Trial Now!
Webinars.com/FREE-Trial

3. Use Digg.com (http://www.digg.com) to come up with killer headlines. Look for the headlines with the most diggs.

750 diggs
⚑ digg

Relieve back pain by drinking more water
davidseah.com — "Apparently I had been turning my hands have also started to fade away. It might be t way I'm feeling." (Submitted by drum_bum)

4. Tie your ad copy to current events.

353 diggs

Economic crisis, meet obesity crisis

latimesblogs.latimes.com — The economic downsi American. (Submitted by gamers403)

digg   101 Comments   Share   Bury   Made po

5. Always split-test ads. Have two ads that look almost the same except for one element. Find a winner and then write a new ad to beat it. Keep doing this again and again to constantly improve your click-though rate (CTR) and conversion rate (CR). Start by testing the big stuff (offers, guarantees, marketing message, etc.) and move down to the small details. Changing one single word can double or triple your CTR, so test everything. Google Adwords CTR Validity Checker (http://www.vertster.com/adwords-tool/) allows you to calculate if you have enough data to make a good decision.

6. Avoid Dynamic Keyword Insertion (DKI). This is a feature that includes your keywords in your ads. I used to love it, but then I realized that it made some of my ads look really bad if the keywords people searched for weren't relevant to the ads. Stick to one keyword and one ad per ad group and you'll do great.

7. Use numbers and special characters in your ad ($, #, ®, ©, ¼, &, etc.) They're a great way to get people's attention.

8. Call your readers. For example, "hey you, skinny man" or "hey you, bankruptcy victim."

9. Use negative ads. For example, "Is Bob's New Book a Scam? Don't Buy Bob's Book Before You Read This."

10. Try news-style ads. For example, "62 Year-Old Woman Happy with Husband's Performance."

11. Try tease ads. For example, "The One Secret to Reduce Taxes by 87%. Get It Here for FREE."

12. Ask questions: "Are You Sick of Spider Veins?"

13. When you write ads for the Content Network, don't include your keywords. Your goal here is to grab people's attention; be controversial, use weird characters and get their attention in any way you can

How to Optimize Your PPC Campaign

1. The best way to ensure you pay as little as possible for your clicks is by using negative keywords effectively (as I mentioned above).

2. Eliminate keywords with no impressions after 7 days.

3. Eliminate keywords with no clicks after 14 days.

4. Eliminate keywords with low conversion rates after 30 days.

5. Eliminate keywords with low CTR or write better ads to increase the CTR.

6. Eliminate keywords that don't appear on the first page or increase their bids so they make the first page.

7. Use the Opportunities feature to get ideas on how to improve your campaign.

8. Put keywords with a lot of traffic in their own ad groups and write special ads for each of them.

9. Use Google Website Optimizer to test elements on your landing pages (headlines, calls to action, graphics, bullets, guarantees, etc.) This is the best way to increase your conversion rate.

10. Pick your winning ads and write new ads to beat the winners.

11. After 45 days, once your campaign has built a good record of high CTR and QS, lower your bids by $0.03 every few days and keep an eye on your traffic to make sure it doesn't drop. Most of the time, once a campaign has a good record you can lower bids without losing traffic.

12. Look for the "Campaign Limited by Budget" message. If your budget is limiting your campaign, set it extremely high. If you absolutely need to have a budget, lower your bids so you get more traffic for the same amount. Lower your bids until the "Campaign Limited by Budget" message disappears.

13. Look for new traffic segments. For example, if you are a chiropractor and a lot of people see you for their back pain, create a landing page addressing that issue and create a new ad group with back pain-related keywords and ads.

14. Compete with yourself. If your campaign is doing great, create a new website (in a new domain) and get almost twice as many leads/sales.

15. Buy several domains. Some domain names get two to four times as many clicks as others. Keyword-rich domains always win. Domains are only $9/year, so buy a bunch of them and see which one has the highest CTR.

16. Don't limit your campaign to Google. Yahoo!, Bing and Ask.com also have PPC programs. They'll send you a lot less traffic, but the conversion rates are usually higher.

How To Ensure an Excellent Quality Score (QS)

QS is extremely important. If you have a high QS, your ads could get twice as many clicks as your competitors while you pay only half of what they pay. In fact, a poor QS is the reason why most people lose money with PPC, so pay attention and follow these guidelines:

1. Have links to a Contact Us page and a Privacy Policy page on your landing page.

2. Include keywords in your ads as much as you can. This is where one ad per keyword makes a lot of sense.

3. Include your keywords in your landing pages, but don't overdo it.

4. SEO factors on your landing page are very important. Have a relevant page title, H1 tag, meta description and meta keywords.

5. There must be a connection between your ad and landing page. If your ad promises a downloadable report and your landing page tries to sell a widget, you'll be in trouble. You can offer whatever you want, just be upfront about it in your ad.

6. Avoid "trouble" words like "offer," "guarantee," "buy now," etc. Put these words in images and call the images 1.jpg, 2.gif, etc. Don't put the trouble words in the images' alt tags either.

7. For all those images that don't contain any of the "forbidden" words, use descriptive alt tags.

8. If you're go after very different markets (such as "beach vacations in Costa Rica" and "ski holidays in Colorado"), create individual landing pages for each of your markets to keep your QS high.

Take Your PPC Campaigns to the Next Level

Google AdWords has many useful features that make your PPC campaigns more successful. Here are my favorites:

Day Parting

For example, you sell pizza. If you bid on the keyword "pizza," your conversion rate probably works well around lunch and dinner time, but does not work well during the rest of the day. If your products sell better during business hours and you ship your products worldwide, you will have an issue with time zones. Because when it's daytime in the US, it's nighttime in Japan. Day Parting is the perfect solution for these challenges.

Search Funnels Reporting

Search Funnels Reporting is an amazing tool that provides you with priceless insight on how your visitors interact with your ads during the shopping process.

Broad Match Modifier

The broad match modifier is an AdWords targeting feature that lets you create keywords which have greater reach than phrase match, and more control than broad match. Adding modified broad match keywords to your campaign helps you obtain more clicks and conversions at an attractive ROI, especially if you mainly use exact and phrase match keywords.

Enhanced CPC

This new automated bidding feature helps you improve your ROI on campaigns with manual bidding. Enhanced CPC uses your campaign's historical conversion tracking data to automatically adjust your Max CPC bid based on the likelihood that your ad will convert. As a result, you should receive more conversions while maintaining or reducing your overall CPA, and spend less time managing your Max CPC bids.

Ad Sitelinks

If you've been paying attention, Google has started showing several links for some sites in their SERPs. A similar tool is now available on Google AdWords.

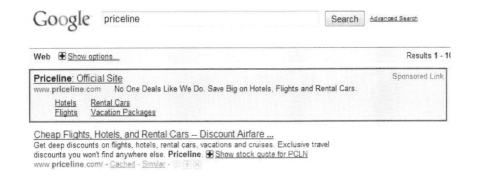

Location Extensions
Location extensions allow you to "extend" your AdWords campaigns by dynamically attaching your business address to your ads.

AdWords Campaign Experiments
AdWords Campaign Experiments (ACE) is a tool that allows you to accurately test and measure changes to your keywords, bids, ad groups and placements.

Remarketing
Remarketing allows you to reach people who previously visited your website, and match the right people with the right message. You can show users these messages as they browse sites across the Google Display Network.

Ten Minute PPC Checklist

Take ten minutes to review the following questions – how can you improve and maximize your PPC campaigns?

- Are you bidding on your competitors' URLs and names?

- Are you bidding on misspelled words?

- Are you including keywords in your ads and landing pages?

- Do you have links to your Contact Us and Privacy Policy pages on your landing page?

- Are you using negative keywords effectively?

- Do you have a low Quality Score (QS)? How can you improve your QS?

- Are you running split-tests for your PPC campaigns?

- Are you using a diverse range of ads? Teasers? News style?

- Are you using attention grabbing headlines in your landing pages?

- Are you utilizing Google Adwords' features such as: day parting, search funnel reporting, broad match modifier, etc.?

CHAPTER 5

SOCIAL MEDIA MARKETING SECRETS REVEALED

Important Note: Watch this Social Media Marketing Seminar I Did:
http://www.theoutsourcingcompany.com/blog/internet-marketing-events/free-seminar-in-portland-social-media-marketing/

I know you probably feel overwhelmed by ALL the social media information that's out there right now. The goal of this chapter is to reveal the secrets behind social media marketing. Actually, social media is not a big mystery but people make it more complicated than it really is.

Do you know why most people fail miserably at social media marketing? Because they don't really get what it's all about. Social media is not about pushing "spammy" sales pitches down your customers' throats. Social media marketing is all about making friends and creating genuine, authentic relationships. However, making friends can lead to future sales.

People like doing business with their friends. If your toilet breaks and one of your friends is a janitor, you'll ask him to fix it. If you don't have any janitor friends, then you ask your friends if they know a janitor they trust. People do business with their friends for two reasons:

- They get a better service, price, deal, etc.

- They give money to people they care about.

How can you apply this principle to social media marketing?

1. Make sure your social media profiles say what you do and link to your site.

2. Make friends. Discover your target market and start talking to those people. Don't sell them anything - just make friends with them and check out their status updates. What are they doing? Is there anything you can help with? Are they asking questions you can answer or looking for something you can give them?

3. After a few interactions, something very interesting will happen. They will ask you the BIG question: "What do you do for a living?" Just tell them what you do, but don't make it sound like you are trying to sell them something. This is where your elevator speech comes into play. This is my elevator speech: "I help companies get thousands of qualified visitors for their websites." Create an elevator speech and be ready to share it when people ask you what you do for a living.

4. People will add you to their "mental Rolodex:" Joan P. - High-end catering services, Marty K. - Real estate agent, etc.

5. When they need a real estate agent, they will call Marty. They will also recommend Marty to anyone who needs a real estate agent (assuming that Marty took the time to build strong relationships with his contacts instead of trying to sell his services).

At seminars, people ask me all the time: "If you could give me only one piece of advice about social media marketing, what would it be?" I tell them to be generous. Give, give and give some more, and a lot of doors will open for them as a result. It's all about "give before you take."

Step 1: Make a List of the Most Influential People in Your Industry

These are the people you want to reach. They have access to tens of thousands of followers and they can help you a lot.

- Search for blogs in your industry, analyze a few hundred of them and keep the ones with the most valuable (and largest) audiences.

- Buy a few industry-specific magazines, make a list of journalists you like and find them online.

- Listen to your audience on forums and Twitter and pay attention to who they talk about.

Step 2: Learn More About These People

I highly recommend using a customer relationship management (CRM) software so you can keep notes of the people you want to network with. I prefer InfusionSoft http://www.infusionsoft.com/

($199/month) but you can use a less inexpensive tool such as HighRise http://www.highrisehq.com ($29/month).

Conduct research about the people you want to connect with. Follow them on Twitter and subscribe to their blogs. For the first couple of weeks, just learn about them and write a lot of notes in your CRM. Your goal is to learn about them and find ways you can help them.

Once you know more about them, send them a personalized request to connect on Facebook and LinkedIn. Make sure you tell them how much you admire them and be very specific why you look up to them (you can mention a blog post you really like or the fact that they make great videos).

Step 3: Keep Your Information Organized

It's important that you become organized in order to follow up with your contacts effectively. You need to separate these industry influencers from the rest of your contacts on Twitter, Facebook, LinkedIn and your RSS reader.

- On Twitter, create a list and put all the influencers of your industry on that list.

- If you use a Twitter client, such as TweetDeck (http://www.tweetdeck.com/) or HootSuite (http://www.hootesuite.com/), create a column and put all industry influencers in that column. I find this easier than doing it directly from Twitter.

- On Facebook you can put all your industry influencers on a list.

- On LinkedIn you can apply tags to your contacts and then filter them by a given tag.

I prefer iGoogle (http://www.google.com/ig) for my RSS reader. Most RSS readers allow you to organize the RSS feeds you subscribe to in folders or tabs.

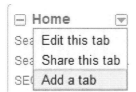

When you're finished with this process, you will have a list of your industry influencers on Twitter, another list on Facebook, another one on LinkedIn and a tab/folder in your RSS reader with all their blog posts. This will make it very easy for you to keep track of them. Your CRM software will prove to be an indispensable tool when you follow more than five influencers in your industry. You should follow at least twenty influencers.

Step 4: Help People

This is the most critical step of the process - help your influencers.

- Subscribe to several blogs in their industries. When you come across cool resources (articles, videos, interviews, tools, etc.), send them to the influencers. Don't send them your content even if it's relevant and useful (this will look self-serving). Send other people's content instead.

- Answer their questions. If they tweet "what's a good shoe store in Manhattan?" research the answer and send it to them. You can even help them when they don't ask any questions. For example, if they post to Facebook "my daughter has a headache," send an article on how to get rid of headaches. Many people approach these influencers asking for something so if you approach them offering them something, they'll pay more attention. You're not expecting anything in exchange; you're just helping others and building goodwill.

- Use SocialMention (http://www.socialmention.com/) to track what people say about them, their companies and their products. Every time they are featured on the Internet, congratulate them. Every time someone says something bad about them on a blog, make a positive comment about that person and then let the person know about the negative comment so they can keep track of it.

- Use SocialMention to track their competitors. Send your industry influencers information on what their competitors are up to, and give them ideas how to improve their businesses.

- Use a tool to detect broken links and run it on your influencers' sites every now and then. Let them know every time you find a broken link. Nobody likes having broken links on their sites, so people will really appreciate it if you let them know about it.

The Difficult Art of Approaching People

Every day I receive a flood of emails from people who want me to partner with them, use their services or hire them. I've been in business for ten years and I've probably replied to maybe one percent of these emails. When one of my employees asked me how she could approach joint venture partners for a project, I thought about the thousands who approached me with offers and the one percent of emails I actually replied to. I realized there are three tricks that the top one percent used that the other 99 percent didn't use.

1. Customize Your Message

Only one percent of the people who approach others with offers actually take the time to know the people they email. They copy and paste the same email to hundreds of people. This is called spam and doesn't work. Sure, you can send millions of emails and someone will reply, but I guarantee that busy people won't waste their time (and those are the ones you want to work with).

In my case, if someone takes two minutes to read one of my blog posts and says something smart about it, he'll be 90 percent in with me. Too bad most spammers waste their valuable time and don't get to know the rest of us a little better.

2. Give Something

The 99 percent group sent me emails asking me for something, and the one percent group offered to give me something. After they offered to give me something, I ended up giving them a lot more in return. I love working with people who think about how they can help me before thinking how I can help them.

3. Be Different

Five years ago, I received a FedEx package with a letter that started with: "I'm writing this letter to tell you why you DON'T want to work with me." Wow, that really caught my attention. The gist of the letter: "I don't follow directions very well. If you ask me to stop working, I won't be able to. It's in me to keep working until my clients are happy. If this is a problem, PLEASE don't hire me." It was funny and different, AND it worked.

The Nuts and Bolts of Social Media Marketing

Social media marketing isn't rocket science and doesn't need to be complicated. The following "nuts and bolts" takes you step-by-step through social media marketing.

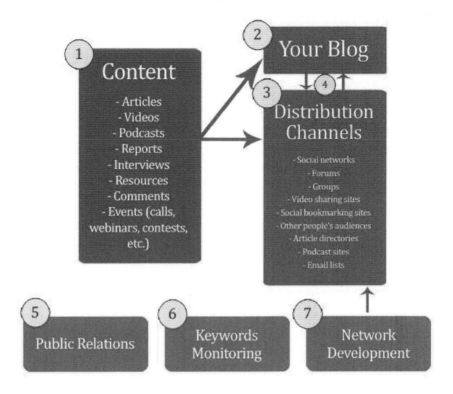

1. Content

- Use common sense to filter out the types of content that won't make sense for your business model.

- Try everything else.

- Measure results.

- Keep doing what works and get rid of everything else.

Most common content:

- Articles

- Videos

- Podcasts (video or audio podcasts)

- Reports/white papers

- Expert interviews (in text format, audio format or video format)

- Resources (these are links to other people's content such as tools, articles, etc.)

- Events (calls, webinars, contests, seminars, giveaways, charity events, etc.)

2. Your Blog

Your blog is the hub of your social media marketing campaign and you want to drive people there. Drive more traffic to your blog by using SEO-friendly tools (refer to Chapter 3).

3. Content Distribution Channels

How to Find Other People's Blogs

You can't post your articles on someone else's blog without their permission, but you can use comment marketing to your advantage. In order to market your company effectively, find out where your target audiences are.

For example, you sell Star Wars merchandise. Google "Star Wars blog." Filter out all the blogs that don't have any traffic. There are basically three ways you can do this:

1. See how many comments each post has. Very few or no comments usually means not many people read the blog.

2. Look for the TweetMeme button. Just a few re-tweets for each post usually means that the blog doesn't have a lot of traffic.

3. Check their estimated traffic on Compete.com.

How to Find Forums (Message Boards or Discussion Boards)

Use these Google queries:

*   Star Wars discussion boards

*   Star Wars message boards

*   Star Wars "powered by phpBB"

*   Star Wars "powered by vbulletin"

Then filter out forums with little or no activity. See when the last thread was started and how many views/replies each thread has.

How to Find Niche Communities

1. Go to Ning (http://www.ning.com) and search for your keyword.

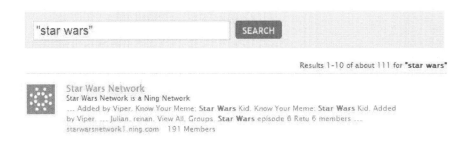

2. Use this Google query: [your kewyord] allintitle:join

3. Use this Google query: [your kewyord] allintitle:"Sign Up"

4. Search Facebook and filter the results by clicking on "Groups."

5. Search for LinkedIn groups by choosing "Groups" from the drop-down list and then enter your keyword in the search box.

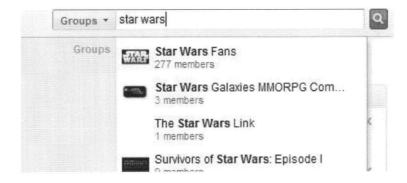

6. Use these Google queries:

[your keyword] social network

[your keyword] online community

Besides blogs, these are the most common content distribution channels:

- Social networks (Twitter, Facebook, LinkedIn, etc.)

- Groups (LinkedIn groups, Facebook groups, Google groups and Yahoo! groups)

- Video sharing sites (YouTube, Google Video, Vimeo, Yahoo! Video, etc.)

- Social bookmarking sites (Digg, Delicious, Reddit, Mixx, StumbleUpon, etc.)

- Other people's audiences (i.e. guest blogging, asking people who have big email lists to broadcast your offer to their lists, asking a blogger to write about your product, etc.)

- Article directories (EzineArticles, GoArticles, ArticleBase, etc.)

- Podcast sites (iTunes, PodcastAlley, etc.)

- Email lists (blog subscribers, people that downloaded your free report, list of potential clients, current customers, etc.)

You will not use all the content distribution channels mentioned above. Discard the obvious ones that don't work for your campaign. For example, you might want to promote your white paper on your blog and on video sharing sites but not on Facebook (and you might want to promote your next webinar using only Facebook Events).

Create a 2-column spreadsheet. In the left column, put a list of your content pieces. In the right column, put your content distribution channels. For every piece of content, decide what channels you'll use to promote your content.

4. Calls to Action

I've discussed the importance of calls to action in previous chapters. Pay attention to your calls to action because it's one of the most important elements of social media. You want to:

- Get people that find your content in the distribution channels to visit your blog.

- Get your blog visitors to follow you through as many content distribution channels as possible.

How to Get People that Stumble Upon Your Content to Visit Your Blog

The short answer is "with a call to action." The call to action should be related to the piece of content they stumbled upon. For example, in your soccer bloopers your call to action could be: "Visit www.mysite.com/blog for more soccer bloopers videos!"

How to Get Your Blog Visitors to Check Out Your Other Content Distribution Channels

The more ways someone connects with you, the higher the chance they will see your content. People who follow you on Twitter, YouTube, Facebook, LinkedIn and are subscribed to your blog RSS feed are more likely to view your content than someone who only follows you on Twitter. Different people prefer to follow others in different ways; give them options and allow them to choose. On my blog, I invite people to subscribe by email, RSS, follow me on Twitter, LinkedIn and Facebook.

5. Public Relations

How to Write an Effective Press Release

The goal of a press release is to attract media attention, and promote your company online. Press releases are another effective tool in your social media tool belt, but they can be difficult to write. Keep these tips in mind when writing an attention-grabbing press release.

Make it Newsworthy

Ask yourself this question: if I were a journalist, would I write a story about this? If the answer is no, find an interesting angle so people will want to write and read about it.

Start Strong

Your first paragraph needs to be strong and clear, and must summarize the entire press release. This is the only part of your press release that most journalists read. If you fail to write a compelling first paragraph, your release is doomed to fail.

Use Correct Formatting

Use this sample press release as a format guide.

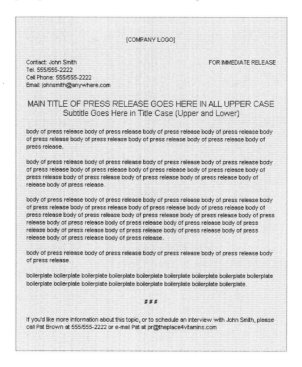

Source: http://www.publicityinsider.com/release.asp

Write an Eye-Catching Headline

The first paragraph is important, but the headline is even more important. Journalists receive thousands of press releases every day. If your headline doesn't grab their attention quickly, they won't read your press release.

Make It Fun and Engaging to Read

The most common mistake is that press releases are boring. Make your press release exciting, engaging and fun to read.

Stick to the Facts

"Cats and Dogs is the best pet store in the world…" won't work. Make your press release as objective as possible. Don't include your opinions – stick to the facts.

Answer Who, What, When, Where, Why and How

These are the six questions journalists address in articles. In your press release, answer the following: who is involved; what happened; when it happened; where it took place; why it happened; and how it happened.

Include Your Contact Information

This may come as a surprise but a large percentage of press releases don't include a direct company contact (i.e. your CEO's information). By the way, journalists want to talk to your CEO, so make sure he/she is available.

Add Resources

Do you have websites that journalists can use as additional resources for your story? Make sure to include these links in your press release.

Keep It Short

One page is the ideal length for press releases.

Consider Deadlines

Pay attention to journalists' deadlines – don't submit your press release past their deadlines.

Check Spelling and Grammar

This is another "duh" piece of advice, but many press releases have misspellings and grammatical errors.

Avoid Jargon

Don't use fancy jargon. Simplify your language. Instead of writing how your new computer has a "HYT567-HN microchip," explain why this new chip is important and how it helps people be more productive.

Use Active Voice

Use "John sold the truck" instead of "The truck has been sold by John."

Get Permission

If you cite a source in your press release, make sure you have their permission to include their information/quote.

Use Mixed Case

DON'T WRITE A PRESS RELEASE IN ALL CAPS! DON'T OVERDO EXCLAMATION POINTS EITHER!!!

No HTML

Don't include HTML code in your press releases – use text only.

Facebook Marketing

With over 500 million users, Facebook is the largest and most engaged social network in the world. However, most Facebook users market themselves poorly. Social media comes down to one simple concept – helping others. Remember this golden rule: "It's not what they can do for you, but it's what you can do for them."

The Don'ts of Facebook

- **Don't Sell** – Don't come across as a "spammy" salesperson. Engage with people and build relationships first.

- **Don't Post Too Often** – A good rule of thumb is to post updates on your Wall two to five times per day. Don't post every hour – that's just annoying and a fast way to lose friends.

- **Don't Mass-Message** – Send out personalized messages instead of the same mass-message to your friends' list.

- **Don't Do Anything That You Wouldn't Do in the Real World** – You wouldn't go up to someone in the real world and say, "Hi, I'm Joe Smith, please buy my products!" Connect with people first and get to know them. People buy from people they know and trust.

The Do's of Facebook

- **Help Others** – Check your ego at the door. Social media is not about you or what you ate for breakfast. Offer your expertise and help. What can you do to make another person's life easier?

- **Build Trustworthy Relationships** – Social media is about building genuine relationships. You can't expect people to just "friend" you; you need to earn their respect and trust.

- **Share Valuable Content** – What's the best way to earn someone's trust? Share valuable, informative content, links, videos, etc.

- **Have Two-Way Conversations** – Don't talk at your friends or fans. Facebook is a two-way street. Actively engage in real conversations with people. Comment on other people's pages and walls – keep the discussion moving!

Four Reasons Why Your Business Needs a Facebook Page

Most Facebook users have profiles. But if you have a business, you also need to create a Facebook page.

- **Liking is Easier** – It's easy for your fans to "like" your page – then their friends see that they "liked" your page (and hopefully, they will "like" your page too!)

- **No Fans Limit** – Facebook profiles only allow you to add 5,000 friends. However, there are no fan limits with pages so the sky's the limit with how many people can "like" your page.

- **Advertising Strategies** – You can implement strategic ads on your page.

- **Send Updates** – When you add links or valuable content, you can send easily updates to your fans in mere seconds.

Three Cool Facebook Tips

1. **Use Lists to Keep Your Contacts Organized** – Remember that not everyone on your friends' list will be interested in the same information. Break down your lists into like-minded groups and segment your groups accordingly: clients, friends, vendors, by city, etc.

2.   **Events Rock** – It's easy to create events for webinars, fundraisers, corporate functions, etc. and then promote to your lists.

3.   **Contests Rock Even More!** – Fun, quirky contests are one of the best ways to generate interest and to increase your friends and fan base. People tell 100 friends and then they tell 100 of their friends. Before you know it, you will have tripled your fans and friends.

Facebook is Not Just Facebook.com

Facebook integrates every application ranging from mobile apps to websites. I suggest using applications on your websites and blogs (see samples below). These apps are also great social proof and make it easier for visitors to share your Facebook pages and profiles.

How to Use Facebook Ads Successfully

It takes time to get Facebook ads right. Test ads to see what works and what doesn't work. Plan on budgeting a few thousand dollars, but once you get the hang of Facebook ads your ROI will be well-worth it.

1. Be Bold

Stand out with your ads. The following ad doesn't use appealing colors, but the ad sticks out and makes an impact. Be quirky and creative with your ads.

Fire your webmaster today and get a website facelift in just minutes! Small business marketing is now simple! Click "Like" below!

Josh Bereano likes this.

👍 Like

2. Test the Heck Out of Everything

Take time to test your ads in order to get them right. Test your headlines, calls to action, copy, images, etc. Choose only one thing to test at a time. For example, if you use a certain image one week, test a different image the following week. Test them side-to-side to see which ad draws more attention and is "liked" more.

3. Optimize for Cost Per Fan (CPF)

You want more fans so don't optimize for clicks.

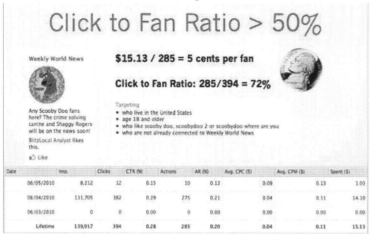

4. Ask People to Like the Ad

In your call to action, ask people to "like" your ad.

Fire your webmaster today and get a website facelift in just minutes! Small business marketing is now simple! Click "Like" below!

Josh Bercano likes this.

5. Link to Facebook Page – Not Your Site

You want people to "like" your Facebook page so don't direct them to an external site.

6. Use CPM - Don't Use CPC

CPM (Cost Per Thousand Impressions) is cheaper than CPC (Cost Per Click).

7. Use Incentivized Likes

Use creative and valuable incentives to get people to click on the "Like" button.

8. Send to Landing Pages and Capture Information

Send visitors to landing pages and ask them to "like" page (Step 1) and then capture their contact information (Step 2).

My name is Tom Ballard and I'm one of the founding members of Free Site Signup. As a business owner and a mentor, I have dedicated my life to helping others find the same success in their lives as I have in my own business. The world of online marketing has opened doors for me that I never thought possible. I work for myself, and I have more time for myself and my family. All of my own success began with a simple affiliate site, and some instruction on how to get setup.

Step 2: "Get Early Bird Notification Of The Live Weekly Webinars"

For those who want to create your own online business, if you have the desire to succeed, you can learn for free with our Live Weekly Webinars! Space is limited so subscribe below to be notified FIRST.

Name:

Email:

[Free Training and More!]

9. Change Your Ads Every 3-4 Days (When They Get to 25% of Original CTR)

When CTR drops to 25% (3-4 days), change your ads. This helps monetize click thru rates.

10. Bid High to Get Ads Approved Faster

With Facebook ads, things happen at the speed of light. Don't wait around for days for Facebook to approve your ads. The trick is to bid high on ads so they are approved faster. After the bid is approved, you can lower your bid.

11. Segment Your Ads

Don't use one ad for all target audiences. Segment your ads and break them down by audience interests, demographics, etc.

Twitter Marketing

Twitter is a micro-blogging platform with over 190 million users who tweet over 65 million times each day. Twitter sometimes confuses people: "What the heck do I do with Twitter and how will it help my business?" I will show you how to easily navigate through Twitter, and how to use it in your favor.

Your Profile

The goal of Twitter is to attract new followers, and the best way to draw people is to create an attractive profile.

- Design an attractive profile background.

- Smiling photos work a lot better than serious poses.

- Include one sentence in your profile that sums up exactly what you do. For example, my profile is straight to the point: "I am a serial entrepreneur and founder of The Outsourcing Company."

- Make sure that you link to your blog and not your website (use http:// so people click directly to your site). Twitter isn't about making the sale - lead people to your blog so you can share valuable content.

Formatting Your Tweets

The most effective way to format tweets is to capitalize the first letter of every word. Include a link and a simple call to action; ask people to retweet. Tweets with links are retweeted 30 more times than those tweets without links. A retweet works like an email forward - people forward your tweet to their followers.

Use hashtags (i.e. #portland and #facebook) which act as keywords. This makes it easier for people to search for your tweets.

CHRISVOSS CHRIS VOSS
7 Ways To Demonstrate True Personal Mental Strength and Build Character Very Inspiring List http://bit.ly/cFHLwz Retweet!
1 minute ago

ZekeCamusio Zeke Camusio
Total Website Makeover: How to Transform an Underperforming Site into the Most Effective Selling Machine - http://bit.ly/bbOzYF #portland
9 Nov

ZekeCamusio Zeke Camusio
FREE Webinar: Facebook Marketing - http://bit.ly/facebook-marketing-webinar #facebook
8 Nov

The Following-Followers Ratio and the Daily Following Limit

Twitter allows you to follow up to 2,000 people. If you go over 2,000 followers, then you are only allowed to follow 10% of that number. For example, if you have 10,000 followers you can only follow 11,000 people. Twitter has a daily new user limit; you can only add 200 new followers per day.

How to Get Quality Twitter Followers

1. Organically - people follow you:

Include your Twitter page URL on your website, blog, newsletter, email signature, content on other sites, business cards, etc.

2. Follow users so they follow you back:

- Search by location
- Search by keywords in tweets
- Search by keywords in profiles
- Follow users who follow the "movers and shakers" (industry leaders, experts in your field, etc.)

Free or Fast

There are two ways you can find Twitter users – free or fast. Search for keywords on Twitter and then add the people you want to follow (free). The other way is to use TweetAdder (http://www.tweetadder.com/). This is paid software that finds and adds people fast. I highly recommend this software as you can run different searches – keywords in profiles, keywords in tweets, locations, etc.

The Most Powerful Twitter Tactic

1. Find the "Movers and Shakers" (industry leaders and experts you want to follow)

2. Follow them

3. Add them to a list (create a separate list for your "Movers and Shakers") – refer to Twitter if you need help creating lists https://api.twitter.com/xd_receiver.html

4. Retweet their stuff

5. Answer their questions (Reply to their tweets and answer questions directly)

Keyword Tracking

1. Use Twitter / TweetDeck.com / HootSuite.com / SocialMention.com to track your tweets.

2. Track the following:

- Your Twitter username

- Your URL

- Your company name

- Your name

- Your competitors

3. Thank your followers for comments and retweets. If you receive negative feedback, respond immediately and handle it in a professional manner.

Scheduling Your Tweets

Every time you post an update, your tweet is added to your followers' timeline. As new tweets appear, old tweets disappear. The more often you tweet, the more people see your tweets. However, it's not a good idea to tweet every hour either.

I recommend using TweetDeck.com to schedule your Twitter updates. The best time to schedule updates is every four to six hours per day. If you don't have a lot of time, seven updates per week is also acceptable (one tweet per day).

Integrating Twitter with Your Site

Just like Facebook, you can also integrate Twitter on your site. I recommend using the following plug-ins for your site. These plug-ins allows visitors to easily retweet and share your Twitter page with others.

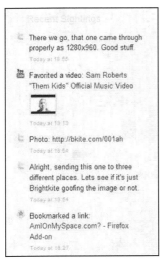

Sexy Bookmarks

LifeStream

TweetMeme

The "5 Minutes a Day Twitter Marketing System"

- **Just Once:**

  o Integrate Twitter with your website

  o Find people to follow

- **Every Day (5 minutes):**

  o Unfollow users who don't follow you back after 3 days

  o Follow users who follow you

  o Follow new users

  o Monitor your keywords and respond

  o Help the "Movers and Shakers" and retweet their stuff

- **Once a Week (30 minutes):**

  o Find content with Google Reader (http://www.google.com/reader) and schedule updates (every 4-6 hours) for the entire week.

LinkedIn Marketing

The best industries that benefit from LinkedIn marketing are companies and entrepreneurs who sell and market directly to businesses. LinkedIn is comprised of companies from across the globe and is one of the most powerful professional networking sites online.

As I mentioned in the Facebook and Twitter sections, people don't want to be spammed. Apply the "no spam" rule to LinkedIn. Develop genuine relationships first. Yes, sales can be the end result of your relationship, but don't initially "sell" to your LinkedIn connections.

How to Create an Attractive Profile

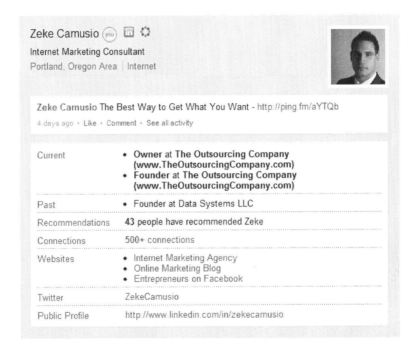

Summary

Zeke Camusio is a serial entrepreneur who loves starting businesses, talking about marketing and enjoying every day of his life.

Zeke has been named "Internet Marketing Expert" by Entrepreneur Magazine and he's the author of Google Rocketship, a Search Engine Optimization book published by Startup Nation, one the most trusted entrepreneurship resources in the world. Zeke is an online marketing columnist at some of the most reputable blogs in the industry, such as Search Engine Journal, PartnerUp and YoungEntrepreneur.

Zeke is the founder of The Outsourcing Company, an Internet marketing agency with three offices worldwide that has helped over 200 businesses skyrocket their sales.

- Include an attractive professional photo.

- Below your name, include your title/how you help people (this is the first thing people will see).

- The next line is your **status update** (similar to Facebook's update). You can share information, post your blog links, etc. in your status update.

- **Recommendations** are great social proof. It's important to ask for recommendations as testimonial to your professional background and credentials.

Recommendations For Zeke

Owner
The Outsourcing Company (www.TheOutsourcingCompany.com)

"I learned alot from Zeke, he is really up to date on all of his information.
It was refreshing to read what a learned and seasoned Consultant had to impart on others.
Thank you Zeke and keep up the GREAT work.." *November 8, 2010*

1ᵗ Bruce W. Davis, *Owner/Associate, Smart World Traveler*
was with another company when working with Zeke at The Outsourcing Company
(www.TheOutsourcingCompany.com)

"Zeke has been an innovative and effective resource of information on Internet Marketing and
Social Media strategy. His blogs and online support have directly contributed to our
successful implementation of a Social Networking Service for our PMI San Diego Chapter
Membership (1300+). I would certainly recommend his services and support to anyone
looking to take advantage of internet and grow their business." *April 25, 2010*

1ᵗ ✓ Todd T. Greenwood, *Vice President of Communications, Project Management
Institute, San Diego Chapter*
was with another company when working with Zeke at The Outsourcing Company
(www.TheOutsourcingCompany.com)

"I have been following Zeke's outstanding articles for the past year and I can without a doubt
that he is someone you should consider getting to know and doing business with!" *April 19,
2010*

1ᵗ Michael King, *Director of Public Relations, Clearly Lasik*
was with another company when working with Zeke at The Outsourcing Company
(www.TheOutsourcingCompany.com)

"I would highly recommend Zeke. His knowledge of the internet is amazing and his
strategies are sound. Zeke is realistic about results and coaches his clients that creating
awareness and driving traffic does take some time and commitment financially. What I
appreciate about Zeke is that he can create a plan that work for your budget even if you
don't have a lot of money. Again, I would highly recommend Zeke." *April 15, 2010*

Top qualities: Personable, Expert, Good Value

1ᵗ Peter Field,
hired Zeke as a Business Consultant in 2009

- **Connections** show how many people are included in your network.

- Under Connections, list your **Websites**. Include keywords in website and blog descriptions. Don't use the defaulted "My Website" or "My Blog." For my links, I used "Internet Marketing Agency" and "Online Marketing Blog."

- Don't forget to include your **Facebook** and **Twitter links**.

- Make sure your **Summary** is well-written and sounds professional. Explain exactly what you do and how you help people.

- Use keywords in the **Specialties** section. Make sure keywords are relevant to your industry/profession. See my Specialties below.

Specialties

online marketing expert, internet marketing specialist, Search Engine Optimization, Social Media Marketing, Pay per Click, Conversion Rate Optimization, internet marketing consultant

---

- **Groups and Associations** are the groups you belong to on LinkedIn.

- **Contact Settings** feature what kind of networking and career opportunities interest you.

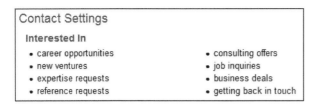

Contact Settings

Interested In

- career opportunities
- new ventures
- expertise requests
- reference requests
- consulting offers
- job inquiries
- business deals
- getting back in touch

- • Make sure you fill out your Profile completely. If your **Profile Bar** is incomplete, you look less professional and makes it difficult for people to find you on LinkedIn.

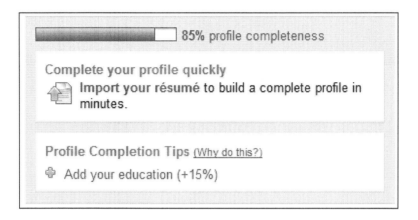

85% profile completeness

Complete your profile quickly
Import your résumé to build a complete profile in minutes.

Profile Completion Tips (Why do this?)
Add your education (+15%)

LinkedIn Marketing Tactics

Tactic #1: Get Recommended

Under your **Profile**, click on **Recommendations**. Choose **Request Recommendations** and choose your contacts, personalize your request message and send your recommendations (you can send up to 200 requests at one time).

Tactic #2: Reach Out to New People

- For example, my goal is to reach out to 5 new people per week.

- I search for 100 profiles a week and find 5 people I want to know better.

- I don't have an agenda – I just have fun! If something comes from it, that's great. Sometimes I make new friends and business contacts, and sometimes I don't. Either way, I have a great time meeting someone new.

Tactic #3: Be a Connector

Do you know someone who is looking for a house in Arizona and you also know a real estate agent in Arizona? Be a connector and help people. Connect two people together who could benefit from each other. Remember that the main goal behind LinkedIn is to help people.

Tactic #4: Join Groups

Join groups that fit your industry and profession. Groups make it easier to network with like-minded professionals with similar interests, backgrounds, etc.. Groups are a great way to share your expertise and get to know people in your field.

In the Search bar, click on **Groups** in the drop-down menu and then enter a search term (i.e. real estate).

LinkedIn lists all the groups associated with "real estate." Browse for groups that are a good match and click on **Join Group**.

Tactic #5: Start a Discussion

Under **Groups**, click on **My Groups.** Pick a group and then under **Actions** choose **Start a Discussion**.

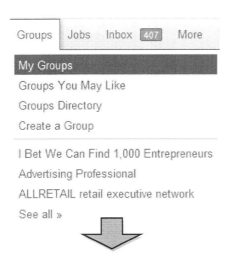

When you start a discussion, write a thought-provoking question as the headline. I like to use group discussions to conduct my market research. Ask for people's input and feedback. I've discovered that people love to be included in the conversation and like to share their opinions.

Tactic #6: Add a Link!

Include a call to action and attach a link to your blog post. Ask people to read your blog post.

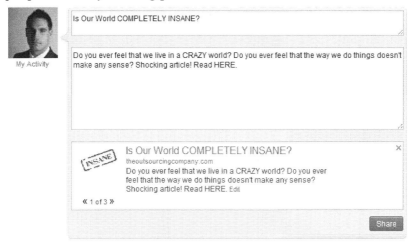

Tactic #7: Start Your Own Group

Under **Groups**, click on **Create a Group**. By creating your own group, you can quickly send special announcements to group members. If you moderate a group with thousands of members, it's an easy way to share information with everyone at once.

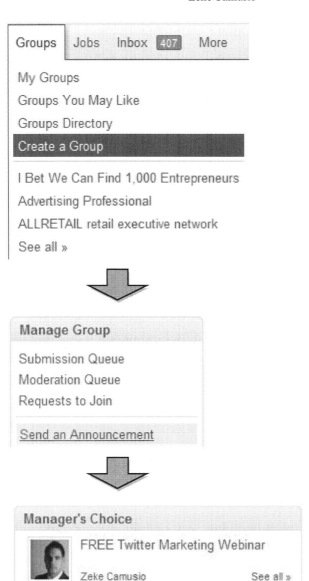

Tactic #8: Grow Your Network

Search for people who share common professional or personal interests. Search by keywords, interests, location, title, company, etc. Remember LinkedIn is about the people behind the accounts. Don't add people just for the sake of adding people. Connect with them in a genuine way – look for common interests or hobbies that you share. I've found a lot of people on LinkedIn who share my love of tennis.

Tactic #9: Answer Questions

Another great way to connect with others on LinkedIn is to answer questions. Share your knowledge and feedback with other LinkedIn professionals. You can filter searches by choosing topics in your range of expertise. If you need help or advice, you can also ask questions.

Under **More**, click on **Answers**.

In the **Answers** section, choose from **Answer Questions** or **Ask a Question**.

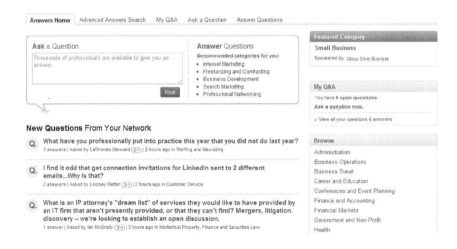

Tactic #10: Promote an Event

LinkedIn makes it easy to promote your webinars, conferences, and special events. Under **More**, click on **Events** and then **Add an**

Event. After you create an event, an event announcement is sent to your connections.

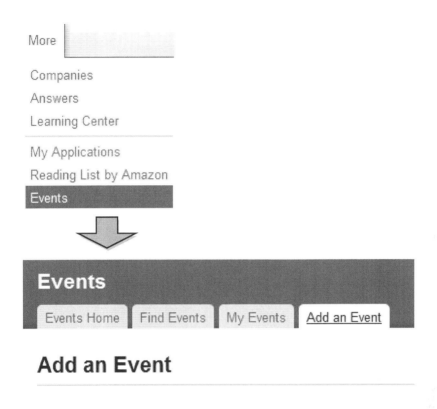

Tactic #11: Link Your Blog and Your LinkedIn Profile Together

Link your WordPress blog and LinkedIn profile (automatically posts blog to your profile). Follow the WordPress set up instructions.

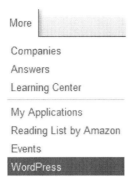

More

Companies
Answers
Learning Center

My Applications
Reading List by Amazon
Events
WordPress

Tactic #12: Meet with Your Local Connections

Take your online networking offline. Search for your local connections and meet with them in person. I've connected with people who share my common interests (i.e. tennis). When I travel for business, I search for people who live in that city and invite them out for coffee. Not all of them have turned into business opportunities, but it's a great way to meet people face-to-face.

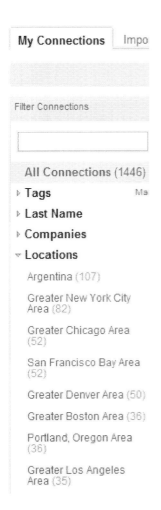

Tactic #13: Promote Your Profile

Promote your LinkedIn profile on business cards, email signature, blog, website, etc.

Tactic #14: Use LinkedIn Ads

LinkedIn Ads (Pay Per Click) are a great way to segment your targeted audience. Get very specific with your ads (company size, seniority, age, and geography). Targeted ads give you a better chance to convert into paying customers.

 Go to LinkedIn DirectAds »

Target Audience 4,075,720 Change

Company Size:	51-200
	201-500
	501-1000
	1001-5000
	5001-10000
	10001+
	11-50
Seniority:	Director
	Manager
	Vice President
	Chief X Officer
	Owner
Age:	25-34
	35-54
	55+
Geography:	United States

YouTube – Viral Video Marketing

When it comes to social media marketing, viral videos are hot. But people fall short when it comes to promoting their videos. The following tips will give you an advantage over your competitors who market on YouTube.

Anyone Can Do a Video

You don't need to be a professional videographer to create a YouTube video. If you have great content, that's all that matters and will land you the most hits. I recommend using **Camtasia** (http://www.camtasia.com/) which allows you to easily record an audio/PowerPoint presentation – an easy way to create a YouTube video.

Learn What Works

There are three types of viral videos that work well on YouTube.

1. Funny – Entertains and makes people laugh

2. Weird – Unique, quirky videos

3. Useful – Videos that help people and make their lives easier

Customize Your Channel

Customize your background, photos, etc. on your channel.

Put Your URL in the Description

Make sure to put http:// in your URLs so people can click on the link.

Put Your Keywords Everywhere

People search vides by browsing categories and keywords. Make sure you put your keywords in tags, descriptions, headlines, etc.

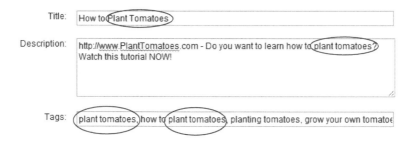

"Steal" Keywords from Successful Videos

Search tags of popular videos. "Steal" those same tags from popular (most viewed videos), and include those keywords in your video tags.

Choose the Best Thumbnail

Make sure to include an attractive thumbnail.

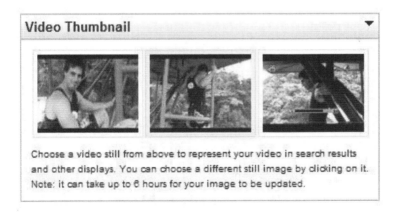

My Account > My Videos > Edit

Use Video Responses

Instead of responding with comments, respond with video responses.

Search your keywords > Find videos with a lot of views > Post video responses where appropriate (don't spam)

In the comments section, click on "Attach a Video" and then "Post."

Create Playlists

Add playlists that will catch people's attention. See instructions below:

Add your video to a new playlist you create > Add other videos > Choose a smart name for your playlist (think keywords)

Offer Valuable Content, Not a Sales Pitch

Do not use YouTube videos to sell your products and services. Think valuable 10 percent content.

Use Calls to Action

It's important to include strong calls to action in annotations (see below). In your calls to action, ask people to do the following: like the video, subscribe to the video and share the video with friends.

In your Calls to Action, invite viewers to:

- Embed video link on their site

- Follow you on Twitter

- Find you on Facebook

- Visit you blog (not website) for valuable content (not sales letter)

Use TubeMogul

Allows you to load videos to multiple sharing sites. TubeMogul (http://www.tubemogul.com) shares analytics about viewers (who watches videos, traffic statistics etc.)

TubeMogul

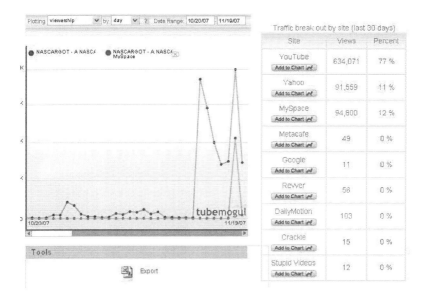

Organize Contests

Contests are an innovative way to engage your viewers. Here are fun contest examples I found on YouTube:

- "Do a 360 with our skis"

- "Plant your own tomatoes using our kit"

- "Show us a crazy way to use our vacuum"

Promote Your Videos Outside of YouTube

- Email contacts, friends, co-workers

- Blog subscribers

- Twitter, Facebook and LinkedIn

- Embed them on your site / blog

- Ask people to share!

Keep It Short!

I recommend keeping videos to around two minutes. Out of all the YouTube testing I've conducted, I found videos that are two minutes and under receive more views.

Analyze & Learn

Your videos might hit it big on YouTube and some might bomb. The only way to learn what's working is to analyze your videos – what are your top performers?

How to Leverage Strategic Alliances Beyond Social Media

Remember that social media is not an island and it takes time to develop valuable relationships. A successful social media marketing campaign does not happen overnight. Facebook, Twitter, LinkedIn and YouTube should not be the only tools in your Internet marketing arsenal. Social media enhances your marketing strategy, but don't solely rely on it to promote your business.

Social media can save you time and money, but it only takes you so far. Don't forget that people still want that personal touch. Phone calls and face-to-face meetings are just as important when it comes to building solid relationships with your customers and clients.

One of my favorite words is leverage. One of the best ways to use leverage is to take advantage of other people's networks. Strategic alliances are one of the best ways to grow your business. Social media marketing can be the catalyst for building these alliances, but take it one step further. Remember it is important to develop beneficial relationships offline as well.

Step 1: Who Buys Your Products/Services?

- If you sell Harley Davidson parts - Harley Davidson owners

- If you're a small business consultant - Small business owners

- If you're a chiropractor who deals with chronic fatigue - Patients who suffer from chronic fatigue

Step 2: What Else Do Those People Buy?

- Harley Davidson owners - Harley Davidson motorcycles, t-shirts, memberships to Harley Davidson clubs, etc.

- Small business owners - Office furniture, printing supplies, web design services, legal services, CPA services, etc.

- People who suffer from chronic fatigue - Red Bull, multi-vitamin supplement, coffee, etc.

Step 3: Create Strategic Alliances with Companies that Sell to Your Customers

- Negotiate with Harley Davidson dealerships so when the motorcycles they sell break, they buy parts from you.

- Work with companies that sell Harley Davidson t-shirts so they give their buyers a $50 gift card to buy your Harley Davidson parts. The other company wins because they give their buyers something valuable, and the customer wins because he receives a gift card. You win because you will get their business.

- Work out a deal with a local web design firm so they offer a free one-hour consultation with you to their clients. In return, email your contacts and let them know this web design agency builds great websites and that your friends will receive a 10 percent discount by mentioning your name. You can do the same thing with local attorneys and CPAs.

- Approach a local coffee shop so they give your brochure to people who buy Red Bulls and coffee on a regular basis. In exchange, give your business to the coffee shop and hold your company meetings there.

Ten Minute Social Media Checklist

Take ten minutes to ask yourself the questions below. What's working with your social media marketing? What tools are missing?

- Are you helping people and building authentic relationships on social media? Don't spam or sell to people.

- Have you created strong social media profiles with attractive photos, keywords, links etc.?

- Are you optimizing your social media accounts with plug-ins on your websites and blogs?

- Are you including calls to action and asking followers to share your links, videos, blog posts, etc.?

- Are you sharing valuable content on Facebook, Twitter, LinkedIn and YouTube?

- Are you using contests and promotions to attract more followers?

- Have you included social media links on your email signature, business cards, blogs, websites etc.?

- Are you meeting face-to-face with your local LinkedIn connections?

- Are you testing your YouTube videos?

- Are you segmenting Facebook and LinkedIn ads to target specific audiences? Which ads work or don't work?

CHAPTER 6

INTERNET MARKETING TACTICS THAT BOOST YOUR BOTTOM LINE

How to Build a Solid Email List in Less Than 90 Days

I love building email lists for one simple reason – they are my assets. If Google decides to change its algorithms and mess with my rankings, I still have my email list. If Google decides to start charging me $10 per click for my Pay Per Click campaign, I still have my email list. Nobody can take that away from me. It also makes me nervous when one of my businesses depends too much on one client, vendor or service provider (like Google).

The beauty of email marketing is that if you build a great relationship with your list and they see value in emails you send them, they'll respect you and respond to your calls to action. That's a smart way to build a strong business.

Before I tell you how you can build a killer (and huge) email list in no time, there's a disclaimer: I failed miserably for two years trying to build a big list myself. It was one of the most difficult tasks I've ever done until I discovered an email marketing formula that really works. I perfected my formula over the past five years, and this technique works in any market/industry.

Step 1. Create Valuable Content

Give people something of value in exchange for their email addresses. These are my favorite "bribes" (in order of preference):

- Reports

- Videos

- Tools

Make the reports short (3-7 pages) and address one specific topic. For example, if you are in the dating industry instead of "All the Secrets for Successful Online Dating" create reports such as:

The One Thing Women Want to Hear from Men on Online Dating Sites

Safe Online Dating: How to Make Sure The Guy You're About to Date Isn't a Pervert

I conducted a lot of testing, and found reports that cover specific topics have a far better response than general reports. Plus, this allows you to create a lot of reports around your topic.

Make reports short. Most people feel if isn't long then it's not any good. That's just nonsense. You can still pack a punch with short reports, so make them concise and to the point. The same advice applies for videos. Make them short and cover one specific topic.

Tools are more expensive but not nearly as expensive as you might think. You can find a designer on Elance (http://www.elance.com) or Guru (http://www.guru.com) to create a tool for you for less than $100. Here are some tool ideas:

- Real estate industry: mortgage payment calculators

- Weight loss industry: calories calculator for different foods

- Legal industry: a tool that helps you figure out how much you should sue someone for

How to obtain email addresses from tools:

- Send results by email (this gives you an excuse to gather email addresses)

- Free and premium versions of the tool (the free one doesn't require registration but the premium one does)

Make sure people don't need to register before using the tool or that will kill your conversion rates.

Step 2. Create Landing Page

Create a landing page where people can download your free report, videos or tools.

- Ask people to make a minimal commitment – don't bombard them with too many requests. Keep forms short (email address only is best), use one-step registrations, don't require email confirmation and don't ask for money.

- Although your stuff is free, it doesn't mean you don't need to sell it. Give people a reason to invest in reading your report, watching your video or using your tool. Use an attention-grabbing headline (include the word FREE) and use bullet points to explain the benefits of opting in. Have an obvious, HUGE call to action with arrows pointing to it. There should be no doubt in their mind what you want them to do.

- For more tips, refer to Chapter Two - How to Create Killer Landing Pages.

Step 3. Promote Landing Page

Drive people to your landing page in the following ways:

- Your contacts: Email your entire address book and ask them to spread the word for you. Give them a great reason to do it.

- Social media marketing: Post to Twitter, Facebook, LinkedIn, etc.

- Forums: Post to the most influential forums in your industry

- Blogs: Approach the most respected bloggers in your market, tell them about your free report and ask them if they're willing to blog or email their lists about it.

- In most cases, you'll need to go one step further: create an additional report and give it to the bloggers for them to give it away to their readers. You won't get any email addresses in exchange for this report, but here's a sweet trick: at the end of that report, mention that you have another great report and tell them how to get it. Most bloggers will be happy to give their readers a free report with no strings attached. Some "famous" bloggers will request that the report is exclusive for them. If the blog has a lot of traffic (check the number of comments, Compete.com or Alexa.com to find out), it's probably worth it.

- Groups: Use Facebook Groups, LinkedIn Groups, Yahoo! Groups and Google Groups to find communities built around your market. Let these people know about your content.

Step 4. Treat Your List (Very, Very) Well

Respect them, send them great content and don't spam them with your specials. A good rule of thumb for email campaigns is 95 percent content and 5 percent promotions.

What Went What Wrong?

- Very few people visited your landing page? You chose a bad title for your report/video/tool, the topic isn't interesting enough and/or you haven't done a good job promoting your content (step 3 of this formula).

- A lot of people visited your landing page but 25 percent or less opted-in? Improve your copy. Review the copywriting tips from Chapter 2 or hire a professional copywriter.

Online Advertising – The Magic Formula That Works Every Time

I create a lot of online advertising campaignsfor my clients, and I found this formula works the best every time.

Step #1: Test A LOT of Sites

When it comes to online advertising, it's impossible to guess what websites will perform best. There's only one thing you can do: test a lot of them. I use these networks:

- **Google AdWords Managed Placements** - You choose the websites where your ads are displayed.

(http://adwords.google.com/support/aw/bin/answer.py?hl=en&answer=99502)

- **Google AdWords Content Network** - Google shows your ads on pages that are related to them. (http://www.google.com/adwords/contentnetwork/index.html)

- **AdBrite** - The biggest ad marketplace on the web (http://www.adbrite.com)

Step #2: Test Everything

- Websites (to see what sites work and what sites don't)

- Text vs. image ads.

- Different sizes for image ads.

- Different headlines and calls to action.

- Different marketing approaches

Keys to effective testing:

- Define your goal. Your goal should be conversions, not clicks or impressions.

- Split-test the same kind of traffic. Don't show Sunday traffic one ad and Monday traffic a different ad. Sunday traffic is different from Monday traffic. The same concept applies for all other variables. Make sure that when you run split-tests you show both ads to similar audiences.

- Achieve statistical significance. This is a fancy term that means "you need enough data to be confident that the results you're getting are accurate."

- Be very organized and document everything. If your experiments are a mess, the outcome will be an even bigger mess.

Step #3: From CPC to CPM

When you first begin, you will use the cost-per-click (CPC) model. That's a good way to understand what websites work and which ones don't work. Once you have a good idea of what websites are losing you money, get rid of them as fast as possible.

The next step is very important. Use the CPM (cost per 1,000 impressions) model for those websites that worked for you in the past. You'll get a lot more clicks and will pay less by using CPM instead of CPC. You can manage this through your AdWords and AdBrite accounts.

Step #4: Cut Out the Middle Man

Advertising networks only pay the publishers about 30 to 50 percent of what they get from you. If you pay $2 for 1,000 impressions, the publisher will get anywhere from $0.60 to $1; the network will keep the rest. Contact the publisher directly and negotiate a CPM price. Offer them 60 percent of what you're currently paying. That will work out better for both you and the publisher.

Step #5: From CPM to Flat Fee

Take a list of those sites that perform great and approach their webmasters. Negotiate a flat fee instead of CPM. They prefer this anyway and you can save a lot of money this way. Plus, your ads can be on their sites 24/7 instead of on/off. You won't need to share the space with other advertisers anymore.

Step #6: From Flat Fee to CPA/Affiliate

- Cost-per-action (CPA) marketing and affiliate marketing are great ways to advertise your products because your publishers will only get paid when visitors complete a goal on your site. The goal could be to submit a contact form, proposal request, download a free report, buy a product, etc.

- When you get your publishers to become your affiliates, they will be more motivated to make your offer work. They'll be more likely to email their lists about your offer, advertise it in their newsletters and give your banners top visibility.

- When you offer your publishers to become affiliates, tell them it's on a trial basis. If they don't make more money that way, you can always switch back to the flat fee model. Show them there's nothing for them to lose, and they'll be happy to try it out.

Affiliate Marketing Tips for Merchants

One of the biggest issues I've seen with merchant affiliate marketing programs is that they lose momentum over time. The program starts off successful in the beginning – affiliates sign up and sales soar. But then referrals and sales drop, or stop altogether. So what happened?

Don't worry that your products or services aren't good enough. Your sales might be slipping based on how your website looks and/or how your affiliate program is structured. Carefully examine your website and the affiliate program itself. What can you adjust and fix to make it work better?

Remember that your affiliate program is a marketing program, and not an advertising campaign. That means you need to manage the program. If you don't have time, hire an affiliate marketing manager to run the program for you. Treat your affiliates like your employees. Monitor their performance, and make yourself available to them when they need help. Keep them motivated through incentive opportunities that help boost your sales.

For more information about affiliate marketing for merchants, I highly recommend these two books: *A Practical Guide to Affiliate Marketing: Quick Reference for Affiliate Managers & Merchants* and *Successful Affiliate Marketing for Merchants*.

CHAPTER 7

ANALYTICS – HOW TO UNDERSTAND YOUR TRAFFIC SO YOU CAN MAKE SMART DECISIONS

Even if you follow all the Internet marketing tips and tools discussed in previous chapters, your hard work could be all for nothing. If you don't measure and analyze, how will you know what works and what doesn't work? Analytics helps you make good marketing decisions based on the data you receive.

Google Analytics

If you haven't signed up for a Google Analytics (http://www.google.com/analytics/) account, I suggest signing up for one. Google Analytics shows your traffic conversion rates and gives you real insight into your marketing and advertising campaigns.

1. Dashboard

The Dashboard is an amazing time-saving tool, and I highly encourage you to use it. You can personalize your dashboard with your favorite reports, etc. Look at the top of the reports page and click "Add to Dashboard" button. On the Dashboard, you can move around reports and set up the Dashboard however you want.

2. Map Overlay

The Map Overlay is one of my favorite reports. It allows you to view your traffic by country (and even by state and city). You can see what countries send you the most traffic and have the highest conversion rates. Remember that a conversion can be whatever you set it up to be (i.e. customers who buy your products, visitors who fill out a contact form, how many minutes a visitor stays on your website, etc.).

For example, if the Map Overlay report shows that the United States brings you 1,700 visitors compared to Brazil's 650 visitors, it makes sense to target US traffic compared to Brazilian traffic.

Then review your conversion rates. Your report shows that China's conversion rate is 0.64 percent, Columbia is 8 percent and Venezuela is 7 percent. You'd want to create a specific landing page for Columbia and Venezuela (because they have the highest conversion rates). Because of its very low conversion rate, it wouldn't be a good idea to create a landing page for China.

3. Traffic Sources

This report allows you to see an overview of your traffic sources. Let's say you put your efforts into a PPC and Twitter campaign in China. Based on your analytics, you find out that your highest conversion rates are U.S. Google and your lowest conversion rates are China's campaigns. Don't concentrate your traffic sources in China; put your efforts into traffic sources that give you the highest conversion rates. In this case, you'd want to concentrate on U.S. Google.

4. Keywords

This report shows keyword conversion rates. If you don't find out what keywords generate traffic and leads, you waste valuable time. Concentrate on four to five high conversion keywords that actually make you money. As mentioned in Chapter 3, it's important to analyze keywords as part of your SEO research. See SEO Analytics below for more detailed information.

5. Top Content

The Top Content report shows you the most popular pages on your website. It also shows the average time a visitor stays on a page. The bounce rate shows how many visitors go to your site and then immediately leave. This report is important because it helps analyze your pages – why people stay on one page longer compared to another page.

1. Top Landing Pages

This report shows you the landing pages where people enter your website. This analytic is important because it helps to know what landing pages bring you the most traffic.

7. Top Exit Pages

These are pages where visitors leave your website which is not necessarily a bad thing. However, if you notice they leave your product page in the middle of check-out, you might want to pay more attention to your exit pages.

8. Goals & Funnels

Your goals can be whatever you want them to be. For example, they could be visitors who stay on your site for more than two minutes or who arrive on your confirmation page. You can also set up multiple goals and assign values to each goal. You could assign a value of $50 for visitors who fill out your contact form. For those who request a brochure, you can assign $5. It's really up to you how you want to assign your goals and values.

9. Intelligence

This is another good report and a good place to start with your analytics. The Intelligence report tells you a lot about what looks weird on your site. For example, you notice a red flag with your traffic. This month you had 10,000 visitors and last month you only had 5,000 visitors to your site. Intelligence is helpful because you can analyze why these strange glitches occur on your site and fix them.

10. Advanced Segments

Advanced Segments help you understand how your traffic behaves. For example, 50 percent of low converting traffic doesn't tell you anything. Where does that traffic come from? However, if you find out that 50 percent of your traffic from Spanish-speaking countries converts low then you can make changes accordingly. In order to increase your conversion rate, it might be a good idea to translate your website into Spanish. Use a combination of "and/or" in your searches and make your segments as detailed as possible.

SEO Analytics

In Chapter Three, I focused on SEO tools and tips to bump your ranking to #1 in Google. However, SEO won't do you any good if you don't analyze what keywords send you traffic and how they convert.

Step 1: Check Analytics to Find Out What Keywords Are Sending You Traffic

Go to Google Analytics (http://www.google.com/analytics/). Click on Traffic Sources and then Keywords.

Make sure you click on non-paid so you only see organic traffic.

Search sent 18,259 non-paid visits via 10,952 keywords

Show: total | paid | non-paid

Pull information from the last twelve months to get as much data as possible. Here is an example of keywords I found for a website I manage (brand-specific keywords are blacked out for privacy reasons).

Keyword ⌄	None ⌄	Visits ↓
1.	▬▬▬	590
2.	▬▬▬▬	323
3.	▬▬▬▬▬	284
4.	i-20 form how long does it take to get	275
5.	▬▬▬▬	209
6.	esl classes	191
7.	▬▬▬	175
8.	toefl preparation course	162
9.	▬▬▬	161
10.	▬▬▬▬▬	155
11.	▬▬▬	144
12.	examen gre	142
13.	english school denver	123
14.	▬▬▬▬▬	114
15.	learn english in denver	102
16.	▬▬	94
17.	▬▬▬▬▬▬	90
18.	english school in denver	81
19.	executive english usa denver	66
20.	english classes in denver	64

I pulled the top 20 results, but you should do this analysis with 100 to 250 keywords. Then export this report to Excel.

Step 2: Find Out the Search Volume for the Keywords on the List

Use the Google Keyword Tool
https://adwords.google.com/select/KeywordTool?forceLegacy=true
with these settings:

Enter one keyword or phrase per line:

i-20 form how long does it take to get
esl classes
toefl preparation course

☐ Use synonyms

▼ Close filter options
Don't show results that contain the following words or phrases (enter one per line):

☑ Don't show ideas for new keywords. I only want to see data about the keywords I entered.

☐ Include adult content in my keyword results

Get keyword ideas

Make sure you use phrase match instead of broad to get a more accurate search volume for your keywords.

Export the results to Excel. Keep just the "Keywords" and "Global Monthly Search Volume" columns.

Step 3: Find Out What Your Current Ranking Is for These Keywords

Use the SEOBook RankChecker tool
(http://tools.seobook.com/firefox/rank-checker/). The idea is to find keywords with the potential to deliver a lot of traffic for which you are ranking on the second page of Google. Think about it: if these keywords are getting you traffic on the second page, imagine the

increased traffic you will get if you rank these keywords on the first page. If you are already on the first page but not at the top of the page, you benefit from ranking higher for those keywords.

At the end of your data gathering process, you will end up with a spreadsheet.

Keywords	Global Monthly Search Volume	Google.com position
esl classes	33,100	6
esl lessons	33,100	18
esl class	22,200	6
esl school	14,800	8
gre gmat	12,100	183
toefl preparation course	2,900	9
study english in usa	1,000	19
examen gre	720	10
toefl preparation courses	480	13
toefl preparation classes	390	17
esl denver	210	5
esl goals	210	11
gre examen	140	12
english classes in denver	91	1
english school denver	91	4
english school in denver	91	4
english classes denver	58	3
gre o gmat	58	2
esl speed reading	46	8
examenes gre	36	5
english language school in denver	28	4
english schools in denver	28	4
learn english in denver	28	7
esl classes in denver	22	1

The keywords in purple are on the first page but at the bottom of the page (positions 6-10). With a little bit of SEO, we should rank them in the top 3 results and get a lot more traffic. The keywords in pink are on the second page (positions 11-20). Some optimization should put them on the first page. Again, the idea is to find keywords that already rank well. Make sure they have a significant search volume and do SEO to get even more traffic from them.

Ten Minute Analytics Checklist

How can you improve your analytics? Take ten minutes to review the following questions.

- Do you have a Google Analytics Account?

- Have you customized your Google Analytics' Dashboard to save you time?

- Have you set up your Goals? Remember that goals can be whatever you want them to be (i.e. visitors who fill out a contact form, etc.)

- Are you running reports for your site's Top Content, Landing and Exit Pages?

- Have you analyzed Intelligence to find the strange glitches on your site?

- Have you reviewed Traffic Sources? What countries give you the highest and lowest conversion rates?

- Are you using Advanced Segments to analyze how your traffic behaves?

- Are you analyzing keyword search volume with the Google Keyword Tool?

- Are you using SEOBook RankChecker tool for current keyword rankings?

Have you analyzed what keywords are sending you the most traffic? Least traffic?

APPENDIX A:
INTERNET MARKETING BOOKS

Call to Action - This book will show you how you can transform your website into an effective marketing tool.
http://www.amazon.com/Call-Action-Formulas-Improve-Results/dp/078521965X/ref=sr_1_1?ie=UTF8&s=books&qid=1266191212&sr=1-1

Changing the Channel - This book talks about the importance of having multiple marketing channels and gives you a lot of great marketing ideas. http://www.amazon.com/Changing-Channel-Millions-Business-Agora/dp/0470538805/ref=sr_1_1?ie=UTF8&s=books&qid=1266191325&sr=1-1

Crush It! - Gary Vaynerchuk teaches you how you can make money doing what you love. http://www.amazon.com/Crush-Time-Cash-Your-Passion/dp/0061914177/ref=sr_1_1?ie=UTF8&s=books&qid=1266190990&sr=1-1 –

Don't Make Me Think - Do you want to make an easy-to-navigate and intuitive website? Read Steve Krug's book!
http://www.amazon.com/Dont-Make-Me-Think-Usability/dp/0321344758/ref=sr_1_1?ie=UTF8&s=books&qid=1266189870&sr=8-1

Duct Tape Marketing - This book will give you dozens of great marketing ideas for your business. http://www.amazon.com/Duct-Tape-Marketing-Practical-Business/dp/159555131X/ref=sr_1_1?ie=UTF8&s=books&qid=1266191083&sr=1-1

Guerrilla Marketing - Trying to grow a company on a shoestring budget? This book is for you. http://www.amazon.com/Guerrilla-Marketing-4th-Inexpensive-Strategies/dp/0618785914/ref=sr_1_1?ie=UTF8&s=books&qid=1266191170&sr=1-1

Inbound Marketing - A smart approach to online marketing, website planning and social media. http://www.amazon.com/Inbound-Marketing-Found-Google-Social/dp/0470499311/ref=sr_1_1?ie=UTF8&s=books&qid=1266191027&sr=1-1

The AdWeek Copywriting Handbook - Copywriting is the most important marketing skill and this is the best copywriting book I've ever read. http://www.amazon.com/Adweek-Copywriting-Handbook-Advertising-Copywriters/dp/0470051248/ref=sr_1_1?ie=UTF8&s=books&qid=1266191126&sr=1-1

The Expert's Edge - A very good read that will teach you how you can position yourself as the #1 expert in your market. http://www.amazon.com/Experts-Edge-Become-Go-Authority/dp/0071495673/ref=sr_1_1?ie=UTF8&s=books&qid=1266191280&sr=1-1

Trust Agents -This book is the social media marketing bible. http://www.amazon.com/Trust-Agents-Influence-Improve-Reputation/dp/0470743085/ref=sr_1_1?ie=UTF8&s=books&qid=1266190952&sr=1-1

APPENDIX B:
ENTREPRENEURSHIP BOOKS

Flying Solo - A great book that will teach you how to balance work and life and how to put your priorities in order. If you're a business owner, you have to read this book. http://www.amazon.com/Flying-Solo-How-Alone-Business/dp/1741144248/ref=sr_1_5?ie=UTF8&s=books&qid=1266 189851&sr=8-5

Go Big or Go Home - Wil Schroter has a way to approach business that makes him unique. Don't even think about starting your own company without reading this book first. http://www.amazon.com/Go-BIG-HOME-Wil-Schroter/dp/1599712741/ref=sr_1_3?ie=UTF8&s=books&qid=1266 205389&sr=1-3

Go It Alone! - Go It Alone! is fun to read, full of stories, tips and step-by-step guides. http://www.amazon.com/Go-Alone-Building-Successful-Business/dp/0060731141/ref=pd_sim_b_6

Ready, Fire, Aim - Michael Masterson is my hero. The guy is a very successful serial entrepreneur and teaches some of the most important business lessons ever in his book. http://www.amazon.com/Ready-Fire-Aim-Million-Agora/dp/0470182024/ref=sr_1_1?ie=UTF8&s=books&qid=126620 5306&sr=1-1

StartupNation - Jeff and Rich Sloan are two very successful entrepreneurs and the founders of StartupNation.com, the #1 online community for entrepreneurs. Their book shares a lot of great stories that will give you the inspiration you need to grow your company. http://www.amazon.com/StartupNation-Americas-Entrepreneurial-Building-Blockbuster/dp/0385512481/ref=pd_sim_b_60

The 4-Hour Workweek - Tim Ferris is like no other guy I know and his book is certainly unique. What I like about The 4-Hour Workweek is how it's all about making enough money to be happy (and then spend the rest of your time living your life) instead of making as much money as you can. This book will make you re-think about your life and priorities. http://www.amazon.com/4-Hour-Workweek-Expanded-Updated-Cutting-Edge/dp/0307465357/ref=sr_1_1?ie=UTF8&s=books&qid=1266190095&sr=8-1

The Art of the Start - Guy Kawasaki is one of my favorite people in the whole world. He's smart, funny and overall a great guy. The Art of the Start has some of the brightest business lessons I've learned in my life. http://www.amazon.com/Art-Start-Time-Tested-Battle-Hardened-Starting/dp/1591840562/ref=pd_sim_b_3

The Big Book of Small Business - I really liked Tom Gegax's approach to business. He talks a lot about being a great leader and building remarkable teams. Highly recommended. http://www.amazon.com/Big-Book-Small-Business-Pants/dp/0061206695/ref=sr_1_1?ie=UTF8&s=books&qid=1266205638&sr=1-1

The Knack - I really enjoyed reading this book. Norm teaches a lot of great business lessons using stories, which makes the book very fun to read. http://www.amazon.com/Knack-Street-Smart-Entrepreneurs-Handle-Whatever/dp/1591842212/ref=sr_1_2?ie=UTF8&s=books&qid=1266189840&sr=8-2

The Toilet Paper Entrepreneur - Mike Michalowicz did a great job writing this book. It's all about how entrepreneurs overcome obstacles and achieve their goals. This book is full of great ideas for the small business owner. http://www.amazon.com/Toilet-Paper-Entrepreneur-tell-like/dp/0981808204

APPENDIX C:
INTERNET MARKETING BLOGS

Chris Brogan's Blog - Chris is one of the most knowledgeable social media experts out there. http://www.chrisbrogan.com/

Copyblogger - The best copywriting blog ever. http://www.copyblogger.com

Daily Blog Tips - Great blog on marketing and entrepreneurship. http://www.dailyblogtips.com/

Dosh Dosh - This blog will make you re-think the way you do marketing and business. http://www.doshdosh.com/

HubSpot - Fantastic blog and filled with practical advice. http://blog.hubspot.com/

Mashable Social Media Blog - A great way to be up-to-date with the social media world. http://mashable.com/social-media/

ProBlogger - If you're a professional blogger, subscribing to this one is a must. http://www.problogger.net/

Search Engine Guide - Another great source for online marketing news. http://www.searchengineguide.com/

Search Engine Journal - Some of the most clever and practical blog posts I've read are here. http://www.searchenginejournal.com/

Search Engine Watch - A great way to be updated on what's going on in the search engines world. http://searchenginewatch.com/

SEO Book Blog - Aaron Wall is one of the most recognized SEO experts in the industry. http://www.seobook.com/blog

SEOmoz -This one is my favorite. I can't believe all the great insight they give away for free. http://www.searchengineguide.com/

Top Rank Blog - Lee Odden is one of my favorite people and a real social media genius. http://www.toprankblog.com/

Yoast - Great blog on SEO, SMM and technology. http://yoast.com/

APPENDIX D:
TOOLS & RESOURCES

Chapters 1 & 2

Google Analytics http://www.google.com/analytics/index.html

Google Website Optimizer
https://www.google.com/analytics/siteopt/splash?hl=en

Rocket Surgery Made Easy by Steve Krug: Usability Demo
http://www.youtube.com/watch?v=QckIzHC99Xc

Chapter 3

Acxiom http://www.acxiom.com

All In One SEO Pack http://wordpress.org/extend/plugins/all-in-one-seo-pack/

Angie's List http://www.angieslist.com

Automatic SEO Links
http://wordpress.org/extend/plugins/automatic-seo-links

Bing http://www.bing.com

Citysearch http://www.citysearch.com

Delicious http://www.delicious.com/

DexKnows http://www.dexknows.com

EzineArticles http://www.ezinearticles.com

Firefox add-on/ Link checker
http://www.kevinfreitas.net/extensions/linkchecker/

Google AdWords http://www.google.com/ads/adwords2/

Google Alerts http://www.google.com/alerts

Google Keyword Tool
https://adwords.google.com/select/KeywordTool?forceLegacy=true

Google Places http://places.google.com/business

Google Voice http://www.google.com/voice

Google XML Sitemaps http://wordpress.org/extend/plugins/google-sitemap-generator

HTML Validator http://validator.w3.org/

IBP http://www.ibusinesspromoter.com

InsiderPages http://www.insiderpages.com

Judysbook www.judysbook.com

Juicy Link Finder (subscription fee) http://www.seomoz.org/link-finder/

Kudzu http://www.kudzu.com

Link Atrophy Diagnosis http://www.virante.com/seo-tools/link-atrophy-diagnosis-tool.php

Local http://www.local.com

Merchant Circle http://www.merchantcircle.com

My Blog Guest http://www.myblogguest.com/

Niche Industry Sites http://www.urbanspoon.com

OnlyWire http://onlywire.com/

Ontolo Tool http://link-building-tools.ontolo.com/LinkBuildingQueries.php

Open Site Explorer http://www.opensiteexplorer.org

Ping.fm http://ping.fm/

PubSubHubbub
http://wordpress.org/extend/plugins/pubsubhubbub/

Qype http://www.qype.co.uk/

SEO Browser http://www.seobrowser.com

SEO Friendly Images http://wordpress.org/extend/plugins/seo-image/

SEOMoz Tool (subscription fee) http://www.seomoz.org/labs/link-finder/index.php

SEOMoz Toolbar http://www.seomoz.org/seo-toolbar

SEOQuake http://www.seoquake.com

Superpages http://www.superpages.com

Target Blank in Posts and Comments
http://wordpress.org/extend/plugins/target-blank-in-posts-and-comments/

TripAdvisor http://http://www.tripadvisor.com

WC3 Link Checker http://validator.w3.org/checklink/

Wikipedia http://en.wikipedia.org/wiki/Nofollow

WordPress http://www.wordpress.com

Xenu's Link Sleuth http://home.snafu.de/tilman/xenulink.html

XML Sitemaps Generator http://www.xml-sitemaps.com/

Yahoo! Directory http://dir.yahoo.com/

Yellowpages www.yellowpages.com **CanPages**
http://www.canpages.ca/

Yelp http://www.yelp.com

Premium Directories (subscription-based)

Aviva.com

BOTW blogs (http://blogs.botw.org/)

BOTW.org

Business.com

DMOZ.org

Gimpsy.com

GoGuides.org

JoeAnt.com

Skaffe.com

StartingPoint.com

Web-Beacon.com

WOW.com

Yahoo.com

Local directories (free)

Acxiom via UniversalBusinessListing.org

Bing Local

Google Local

InfoUSA.com

Localeze.com

Yahoo! Local

Yellow Pages.com

Yelp.com

Niche directories

Top 30 niche directories.

Blog directories

BOTW blogs http://blogs.botw.org/

http://www.blogcatalog.com

http://www.blog-search.com/

http://www.blogarama.com/

http://www.blogbunch.com/

http://www.blogcatalog.com/

http://www.blogcode.com/

http://www.blogexplosion.com/

http://www.blogflux.com/

http://www.bloggernity.com/

http://www.bloghop.com/

http://www.bloghub.com/

http://www.bloglisting.net/

http://www.blogrankings.com/

http://www.blogtoplist.com/

http://www.britblog.com/

http://findingblog.com/

http://www.geekyspeaky.com/links/

http://www.getblogs.com/

http://www.globeofblogs.com/

http://www.iblogbusiness.com/

http://www.lsblogs.com/

http://myblog2u.com/

http://www.quickblogdirectory.com/

http://sportsblogs.org/

http://www.theweblogreview.com/index.php

http://www.weblogalot.com/

Chapter 4

Digg http://www.Digg.com

Google Adwords CTR Validity Checker
http://www.vertster.com/adwords-tool/

Google Adwords Keyword Tool
https://adwords.google.com/o/Targeting/Explorer?__u=1000000000
&__c=1000000000&ideaRequestType=KEYWORD_IDEAS#search
.none

Google Traffic Estimator Tool
https://adwords.google.com/o/Targeting/Explorer?__u=1000000000
&__c=1000000000&ideaRequestType=KEYWORD_STATS#searc
h.none

Google Website Optimizer
http://www.google.com/websiteoptimizer

Quintura http://www.quintura.com

SpeedPPC http://www.speedppc.com

Spelling Typo Generator
http://tools.seobook.com/spelling/keywords-typos.cgi

SpyFu http://www.spyfu.com/

Synonyms http://www.synonyms.com

Thesaurus http://www.thesaurus.com

WordTracker Free Keyword Tool
http://freekeywords.wordtracker.com

Chapter 5

Camtasia http://www.camtasia.com

Compete http://www.compete.com

Facebook http://www.facebook.com/

Google Reader http://www.google.com/reader

HighRise ($29/month) http://www.highrisehq.com/

HootSuite http://www.hootesuite.com/

iGoogle http://www.google.com/ig

InfusionSoft ($199/month) http://www.infusionsoft.com

LinkedIn http://www.linkedin.com/

Ning http://www.ning.com/

SocialMention http://www.socialmention.com/

TweetAdder (subscription fee) http://www.tweetadder.com/

TweetDeck http://www.tweetdeck.com

Twitter http://www.twitter.com/

Twitter lists https://api.twitter.com/xd_receiver.html

YouTube http://www.youtube.com/

Chapters 6 & 7

A Practical Guide to Affiliate Marketing: Quick Reference for Affiliate Managers & Merchants
http://www.amazon.com/Practical-Guide-Affiliate-MarketingReference/dp/0979192706/ref=sr_1_2?s=books&ie=UTF8&qid=1287778508&sr=1-2

AdBrite http://www.adbrite.com

Elance http://www.elance.com

Google AdWords Content Network
http://www.google.com/adwords/contentnetwork/index.html

Google AdWords Managed Placements
http://adwords.google.com/support/aw/bin/answer.py?hl=en&answer=99502

Google Analytics http://www.google.com/analytics/

Google Keyword Tool
https://adwords.google.com/select/KeywordTool?forceLegacy=true

Guru http://www.guru.com

SEOBook RankChecker Tool
http://tools.seobook.com/firefox/rank-checker/

Successful Affiliate Marketing for Merchants
http://www.amazon.com/Successful-Affiliate-Marketing-Merchants-Collins/dp/0789725258/ref=sr_1_15?s=books&ie=UTF8&qid=1287778508&sr=1-15

Additional Resources

Balsamiq Mock Ups http://balsamiq.com/products/mockups

Mail Chimps http://www.mailchimp.com

Wibiya http://www.wibiya.com

 **About The Author**

Zeke Camusio is a serial entrepreneur and founder of The Outsourcing Company, an Internet marketing agency with three offices, 17 employees and over 75 clients all over the world. Zeke has started seven businesses (four of them very successful) and has helped over 200 companies make millions of dollars using Internet marketing.

Zeke is a marketing speaker, published author and a columnist for some of the most reputable publications in the industry, such as Entrepreneur.com, Search Engine Journal and Startup Nation.

Made in the USA
San Bernardino, CA
26 October 2014